# VERSES
# AND
# VISIONS:

## Unknown Paths

John T. Eber, Sr.

MANAGING EDITOR

A publication of

# Eber & Wein Publishing

Pennsylvania

Library of Congress
Cataloging in Publication Data

ISBN 978-1-60880-009-4

Proudly manufactured in the United States of America by

Eber & Wein Publishing

Pennsylvania

# Foreword

As I read through many of your comments and personal statements, I couldn't help but notice one word that was regularly mentioned: Outlet. Where many of you indicated how poetry provides an outlet for creativity and honing in to improve one's writing ability, others claim it is an outlet to escape pain, sorrow, or everyday stressors. And even a small number confess how writing a poem is a personal cleansing process with nothing but a purely cathartic purpose. But whether indicative of a creative outlet or a therapeutic one, I found the imagination, motivation, passion, and raw emotion behind the verses in this collection truly remarkable. The nice thing about such an outlet is that it encourages repressed feelings and emotions to surface and even instigates new approaches to past events— for example, what once triggered painful, melancholy feelings might later welcome witty, lighthearted humor after a period of reflection. Or just the opposite may happen when experiencing tragic loss or the death of a loved one. Although poetry shouldn't always be limited to just personal experiences, such experiences shared in this volume are quite moving, and we are honored to publish them. I can't say how many times I've been told that poets draw a great deal of inspiration from reading other poets' work and how even a secondhand witness of their experiences can be powerful and influential. I hope this is the case for you and that you find all of the poems in this volume worthwhile. As a teacher, I always stressed to my students that there is nothing more refreshing, invigorating, or educational than for a poet to read another poet's work. Poetry is a craft to be shared and you have ultimately provided us and each other with small glimpses of the world as it exists through your eyes. Continue to be free and let go!

John Eber Sr.

# Eternal

Like a gentle breeze
To your skin
Makes your body tingle
Like snowflakes fall
Through the night
Makes you long for another
Like a light shower of rain
In the afternoon
Makes you want to dance
Like the sun shining
In the morning
Makes your heart smile
Like the stars sparkle
In the twilight
Makes your lips lonely
Like the sands of time don't run out
Like the wheel of life doesn't stop
Like my love for you is *E.T.E.R.N.A.L.*

Angeline Bailey
*Mineola, NY*

## Mother Nature

It's Winter now, it's cold; the trees
are bare, stripped of their leaves,
red-green and gold, it's time to rest.
She softly said, "Sleep for a little while,
soon Spring will be here,
the trees will burst out again with
all their glory. The little birds awaken
in their nests singing and telling their story.
The flowers will be blooming and the bees
busy pollinating with zest. Love is in the air."
Mother Nature is at her best.

Mary Bruno
*W. Haverstraw, NY*

Although born in Mexico to a Mexican father and an Irish mother, I was reared in England from the age of 1 1/2 years old. During WWII I met my husband and moved to America. We have two children, a girl named Mary and a boy named Frank. My Inspiration for this verse was a two-and-a-half-hour bus ride to get to the city, and my imagination was rampant with ideas. The countryside and the names of the streets all had my mind and heart going. I promised my husband that one day I was going to write my thoughts down. I think now is my opportunity to keep my promise and get to it. I really enjoy sharing my thoughts with someone else; it gives me a great deal of joy.

# Tears

Tears like a warm summer rain help cleanse the heart and soul.

They give you the knowledge that when we wake the next day,
The fresh smell of that summer's rain, reminds of us of the beauty
God created and never meant for us to mourn the living or loved
who have left us.

Each season passes and we wonder what we're meant to do; we
question our motives of the past and the plans for the new. We
forget to let the past be gone and start out new like with the
Wonderment of all that is out there to capture, because we can't
close the door that says yesterday is gone and tomorrow has not
arrived and today is where I am and where the new beginning
is going to start.

Just as the leaves change colors and the snowflakes fall from above,
We go on living and wondering what if? Shed the tears and let the
beauty of our friends and those we love and love us
Bring that last tear we shed for all the yesterdays.

Flow my tears, cleanse my heart and soul, let the pain drift
Away just as I have wiped the last tear.

Rose Bayerle
*Sioux Falls, SD*

# When I Tried to Stop

I'm drowning in its resistance
I need its existence
When I'm on it I fly high
When I haven't used I soar low and crash hard
I need its taste
Its use in me, the faint colored powdery
substance is more than that.
It's life to me
To my…other side
I try to break through ice
To not crash, to not fly high
To live without the addiction
for it to live without me.
This drug is so strong
It's bringing me down
way down low
lowest I've ever been.
My body finally crashes
It crashes hard this time around
So hard I stop breathing, no heartbeat.
I don't have to dream. I don't need to walk
I lay still and never talk.

Kasey G. Shifflett
*Waynesboro, VA*

I started writing poetry and short stories when my parents divorced. It was a hard time, but now I understand it's okay to let go of the past pain. I'm currently attending Wilson Middle School and I love it. I have great friends and awesome teachers. No matter what I go through or where life takes me nothing can slow my writing down. Ellen Hopkins' book, *Crank*, actually inspired me to write this poem. Drug abuse is a big and emotional subject. Sometimes you have to let those feelings out. I just expressed mine in my writing.

## Woe Is My Toe

While walking along,
merrily as I will,
something swoocky
gave me a nasty spill.
It was ooo, yac, akk,
and woe!
The swoocky something
was attached to my toe.
It smelled kind of whoof!
and looked much the same.
It was the type of art,
you wouldn't want to sign
with your name.
I walked a little farther,
and pulled out my chiff.
I tried to wipe it off,
and tried not to sniff.
Now, it wasn't dog poop,
nor birdy drop doo.
It was only a stale sandwich,
became stuck to my shoe.
Woe is my toe!

Carol Owens
*Brooklyn, NY*

Greetings in Jesus' precious name. I was born in Virginia. I was raised in church and still remain so. I've always loved people from all walks of life, both young and old. I truly believe in my love for others and the desire to make them smile. I believe poetry is what God gave me to do so. This written word comes from my spirit and my inspiration comes from God. May God bless my son, daughter-in-law, and grandchildren.

# Travel Quandary

To go on a trip is a daunting affair
I can't leave home with just nary a care
Who will take care of my garden, I wonder
On my return will it look like it's been torn asunder

The mail will pile up each and every day
No one to answer it since I've gone off to play
The bills will remain unpaid for a while
Maybe those I owe will just think that's my style

We are told our home is our very own castle
So why, when I leave, is it such a hassle
But to travel is risky, I beg you to believe
My luggage, if lost, isn't easy to retrieve

Wherever I go, I can be sure of one thing
There will always be something I forgot to bring
The money may run short, the food may be inedible
My touted accommodations may be less than incredible

So, is it better to go or better to stay
Since there's no right answer, I'll do it my way
I'll seize my chances to see the world in its glory
Each new adventure that unfolds can add to the story

After the rigors of travel I know my home will await
It's my refuge, my respite, my place to create
So make the best of both worlds is my advice to you
What a wonderful way to live life till it's through!

Elizabeth Weston
*Tucson, AZ*

## My Three Loves

While I sit and wonder what fate has in store for me
For three great loves have I had in this past half century
All great beauties I've loved so intensely
First Rita whose love for fifty-one years she shared so happily with me
But then God took her back to Heaven to be part of His family
Even now the memory of her love has never dimmed for me
Then one night in a dream she whispered, "Dear Arthur, I now set you free"

Katrin, my second love whose first name less letters K and N spell Rita, strange don't you agree?
For love to happen in one split second was so unexpected
But her true love that I hoped for could never be
Her love, all one-sided was not meant for me
That love is for someone else in her future to meet approvingly
However, Katrin, remember Father Time does not wait for anyone, maybe you especially

My third love is for my granddaughter, Angela Rhae
Whose only thoughts are being mischievous and to play
She first captured my heart in 2006 the first day in May
So there you have my three loves up to the present day

But wait, how thoughtless and forgetful of me
There is a fourth love I call Vergil sometimes Schnooksie
This four-legged creature shows her love every day you will agree
By leaving a little dead mouse on the back step just for me

Art H. Holmes
*Milanville, PA*

I've been so fortunate in my eighty-five years to have known these two beautiful women plus a pretty granddaughter, who is a real pixie. I've also been fortunate to have my companion Virgil, a meowless cat.

## The Life

Life is so good,
Life is so great,
Life is a party,
That everyone must celebrate!
Everyone should tell God,
Thanks for this wonderful gift,
Because without God's help,
Our lives wouldn't exist.
The sun shines,
Gives color to our lives,
The rain constantly refreshes our minds.
The wind blows into the trees,
And honey comes straight from the bees.
The moonlight comes out onto the night,
The stars shining bright on the skies.
Flowers and birds,
Are over the place,
Everything made so perfectly, made with love.
Because everything was created by God our Lord.

Julieta M. Poco
*Philadelphia, PA*

I was born in Portugal and I came to the United States of America in 1989. I became a senior citizen in 2000. I love to write poetry. One night in November 2008 I could not sleep so I got up and wrote this poem.

## Wedding Day

To meet you at the altar,
How I prayed for this day.
A new life together,
in each and every way.
The road is long and full of life,
for today we became man and wife.
My partner, my life long friend,
We will be everlasting to the end.
So I pledge my heart and say I do
to the one I love so pure and true
I dedicate my body and soul to you.

Vanessa O'Sullivan
*South Richmond Hill, NY*


## Jack Frost

What lovely lace
Jack Frost makes!
Tiny snowflakes
Perfect crystal shapes
'tatched to my windowpane.

Oh lovely lace
so full of grace!
Can you survive
The melting pace
before it turns to rain?

Susan E. Schwedler
*Bay City, MI*

# Where Love and Dreams Abound

Here I am again on the road where
love and dreams abound—

I can smell the fragrance that only comes
from no other place around
How truly we never know, to hold
a moment forever is rare—

I would go in and stay and dream

The dreams again, if only I dared
I can see you sitting there with
toys and children on the floor—

Here I am again but darling it's sad

We don't live here anymore—
Where love and dreams abound

Gloria Colbert
*Covington, GA*

# Feeling Her

I didn't believe in that fateful word
Coming from my mouth it was rarely heard
I never once thought it could feel so clear
The feelings that I have make it truly real

I would do almost anything, to make her fall for me
I'd climb the highest mountaintop, I'd swim across the sea
You may think this childish, that's why you cannot see
I've fallen for an earthly angel, that's how much she means to me

Her name will not be spoken her type is truly rare
She has beautiful bright eyes, and silky smooth black hair
Her smile is like a thunderbolt, a chill runs down my spine
Her laugh is like a siren's call, I wish that she was mine

I would do almost anything to make her fall for me
I'd climb the highest mountaintop, I'd swim across the sea
You may think this childish, that's why you cannot see
I've fallen for an earthly angel, that's how much she means to me

By the time you finish reading this, you might likely find
That feelings are complex things, but can be put in rhymes
And that the word I once talked about in the lines above
She makes believe much easier that feeling is called love

Daniel Zeikle
*Polo, MO*

# Happiness

You run around and twirl.
You look like a big whirl.
I see you laughing, jumping and screaming,"Yes!"
Is this your form of happiness?
My happiness is as dim as the last light of the night.
And as I grow older my light ticks and soon click my happiness is gone
forever.
I will never be able to run and twirl and look like big whirl
As you once did when we were once upon a happiness.

Sefiyetu Abdullah
*Tallahassee, FL*

# Love

Sprinkles of rain
Douses its feelings,
Its heat tucked away
In a box of pictures.
While the sun is covered,
Its brightness
Weakened.
The two flowers dance,
But then fade away,
Drooping.
Two in love,
No longer loves again…

Angelique Aucoin
*Mansfield Ctr., CT*

## Treasures

I vision in the hearth fire's ruddy glow
the flame of youth that flushed a maiden's cheek,
and from the embers, crackling so low,
it seems that I can hear her soft voice speak.

The firelight plays upon the walls, and there,
bewitching in its waves of radiant hue,
I see the flowing luster of her hair,
More gorgeous than the flowers she once grew.

The fire's soft warmth reflects her gentle touch,
the reassurance of her lovely smile.
These are the things I miss so very much,
the luxuries I enjoyed so short a while.

In evenings calm I feel her presence near
and see her in the shadows everywhere.
These are the hours I hold to me most dear;
they are God's answer to a lonely prayer.

To some these may seem idle dreams, but I
treasure them more than anything on Earth.
They represent jewels one could never buy,
and I alone can estimate their worth.

Ross G. Stammer
*Chicago, IL*

# What Would She Say?

I have a sister. Her name is Megan. I never know
what's going through her head. She is eighteen years
old and has autism so that just makes this harder!
This is what I think she would say if she could say
what she wanted to say. "Hi, my name is Megan.
I have a sister who talks too much, a mother who
always takes care of me, and a daddy who loves me a lot.
I have a step-dad who can talk like Donald Duck, a friend
of my daddy who's very nice. I have two awesome
grandmothers and I love my Papa!" She would say,
"I go to a special school. I have many friends. I love
playing with my sister's Game Boy. I hate the vacuum.
I hate brooms and I hate the sound of crinkling bags. But,
most of all I love my Papa!" And say, "I hate it when
people talk on the phone. I love playing with phone books.
I hate new clothes. I have a routine and I draw in scribbles.
But I will always love my Papa!" And say, " I love things
that are soft. I love to play in and drink water. I love to
eat spinach and I scarf down mashed potatoes. I love to play
with my mommy's and sister's hair. But, most of all, I
love my Papa!" And say, "I wish I could be like other teenagers.
I wish I didn't have super sensitive hearing. I wish I could be
like everyone else. I wish I could out talk my sister. But,
most of all I love my Papa!"

Shannon K. Thomas
*Severn, MD*

Hello world! As you know my name is Shannon. This poem is about my sister Megan.
She is now 19 years old and has autism. As you can tell, her favorite person in the world
in my mom's dad, Papa. They have a connection that is like no other and cannot be
described with words.

## To Be a Bee

What is it like to be a bee?
You get to live in a honey tree.
You can fly from here to there;
and flowers are everywhere.
Making honey as fast as a bunny;
Working in the hive,
that's enough energy to jive.
Maybe…
it's not that easy

Jillian Vontver
*Bellevue, WA*

## Untitled

Vengeance is mine thus saith thou Lord
Hate and vengeance or that of the Shepherd
Not the sheep
So let my love for thou Shepherd
In my heart and soul run deep

Shepherd speaking
"My hate and vengeance not complete
Even with your headless body at my feet
And your castle walls have fallen in defeat
And in the flame of hell
Satan you do meet!"

James E. Waldrip
*Watsonville, CA*

## Caress

To open one's mind,
violence and pain isn't the answer.
Love the behavior modifies,
opens more minds and doors
than your fingers can count
on this year 2000 if you still
can't settle your disagreements.
It takes a surgeon to fix history's ills—
in a body of a person trying
to hold it all together—sometimes
on paper, sometimes in the sky.
Sometimes it becomes so volatile,
it takes all their might with
much rest and thinking to stop the
hurtfulness "they" inflict on one another.
Only they know who "they" are.
I think the answer is taking
the ills (finding a cure) because
the ills are more valuable and what is wanted.
How can you be ill and accomplish
important things when that's when
it seems it can be done—accomplished.
The "da" of operations has to be repaired
because it causes much damage but also seems
to be wanted even though it is thoughts
without explanation.
It is very hard to pass this "da."
I grew up living in the "da" and when I came
out later in life I found it very hard to cope.

Mary Millo
*Bronx, NY*

What inspired me to write "Caress" was the inner conflict going on within the group of people I had been working with. Because of the weight of responibility given them, they seemed to forget how intimacy had helped to defuse many arguments and disagreements. They were shouldered with children with disabilities and work very complex. These ills they were assigned to led to greater accomplishments. The exhaustion of taking care of this made them fight because it was easier than working things out and they needed to be reminded that love was a diffuser or a distraction. I am 58 years old and have been striving to not be ordinary. I am at a time in my life where I'm trying to take my ambitions to the next level.

## Cancer Denial

It's been a few years
And, inevitably, and then goodness too
I don't walk around frozen and shocked
By the revised expectations of four score and twenty
I don't want to think about it
And it doesn't help me to think about it
And certainly no one else thinks much about it now
And probably was never inclined to ponder it much then,
If the interactions and dialogues were an indication.
Still, people were not unkind
And the bromides proffered, and scraps of consolation,
Uncontroversial, had their bit of truth.
It's no one's job to point me toward the maw
I've hung around near there far too long already.

Shelia Turken, M.D.
*Hastings on Hudson, NY*

# Marvelous Poem

When I come home
I lay down
My little kitten
Makes a big pound

When I get up
To see what's the matter
He's downstairs
With a big platter

My dad comes home
I ran out of sight
Just in time
To see a big fright

I walk in
As if nothing ever happened
And see my dad
Lying on the platter

As he got up
I started to giggle
He doesn't know why
He started to wiggle

As it turns out
The kitten was there
He started climbing
Up his underwear

Megan Hazelton
*Reckville, PA*

## The Birdfeeder

Tessie feeds the birds
All kinds every day
Morning, noon, and evening she fed them

Bits of sweet rolls and pizza scraps
Pieces of apple and hard crunchy toast bits
Peanut butter was a tasty treat

One morning her lifespan came to an end.
The birds came to the feeding porch
Nothing was there, oh well, never mind

The birds went out on their own
They soon found blades of grass
and seeds and juicy worms

The old woman was gone
Merely a vapor on the winds of life
The birds had forgotten the one who loved them so

So it is with all man kind
Too soon good deeds are forgotten
But this one who fed the birds does not care
She is feeding many birds in heaven

Yvonne Bittle
*Charleston, WV*

## What's in a Name?

Who is that character in the window,
The one with the dopey smile?
He looks so lost and bewildered,
And should find a place to hide.

They say his name is Gizmo.
Can that really be a name?
He does have peculiar features,
Yes, they do all look the same.

Why don't we call him Sabatian?
It certainly has a nice ring.
It might make him more cheerful
And might even get him to sing.

Now that we've agreed on Sabastian,
It's really a joyful name.
It might make him very happy
And might even remove some shame.

And now that he seems to be different,
The proper change did take quite a while.
But he's an entirely new person,
No more Gizmo or that dopey smile.

John Favicchio
*Flushing, NY*

# Stop Talking... Start Walking

Why do I stretch?
Why do I walk?
Why so involved with exercise talk?

Well, it's great for my lungs—
And, it's great for my ticker—
Nothing can put me in top shape quicker!

Walking feels so healthy
And it looks so neat—
The swinging of arms
Plus the lifting of feet.

The molding of muscles
the firming of form
The filling of lungs
And the sweating a storm.

Stress-walking keeps me young
Health-walking keeps me loose
Fitness-walking tightens my stomach
While, Race-walking shrinks my caboose.

So why do I walk?
So why do I stride?
For the very best reason—
WALKING keeps me alive!

Richard L. Harding
*Clinton, MA*

# Why

Can anyone answer the question why
Things happen in life that make you want to cry
Why is a question that is often asked
But the answer many seem to pass
Pinpointing the reasons why sometimes is a good thing to do
But not always knowing why can be beneficial too
But nevertheless many individuals set out on a quest
Believing that knowing why will help them pass the test
The test of life itself
The test of personal gain and wealth
Why a three letter word with so much power
A word that is asked at least twice every hour
Searching for the reasons why can drive you crazy
So forget the reasons why and hold onto your sanity

Kalonie Smith
*Los Angeles, CA*

## Now Entering Hope

Tidal waves of blue and green
Pull at my feet and gently caress the golden sand
Rays of red and yellow shine down from the flaming star
we call the sun. Puffs of white cotton balls stretch out
across the sky. The summer breeze laughs along with
the joyous trees that sway in its essence.

Slowly and surely,
Sweet rain drops dance around the earth
And kiss the faces of all who want it
The soft, golden sand spins along with me
As I twirl in the ambiance of the nature.

I allow myself to fall into the crisp waves of the ocean's water
I float along the current
Allowing it to lead me to wherever it wishes to take me
I find myself on a new land.

A land of freedom
A land of peace
A land of love
A land of hope

I like this new land of mine
I think I shall say
Take my hand and join me
Join me and be free
Only one rule in this land of mine:

Eliminate All Amounts of Negativity

Julissa Cardenas
*Santa Fe Springs, CA*

This poem was actually a pretty big thing in my life at the time. I was going through
some speed bumps and a lot of my poetry had become negative. But when I re-read them,
I realized that wasn't me, so then one day I decided I needed to have a positive outlook
on life, hence the title, "Now Entering Hope." See this is my poem! For anyone who is
having some slight rug burns in the carpet of life, I hope this brightens your day.

## Honor's Deflection

Honor journeyed awhile with her plan (and a smile),
She, the model of envied perfection,
But espoused to a louse often gone to the house
Of the woman who held his affection
Stirring deep in her bowels lay a current aroused,
Spilling forth her husband's rejection.
And now time has allowed him no more such beguile,
As she travels the road to correction.

Penelope H. White
*New Kensington, PA*

## Believe

When you "Believe" you represent the inspirational word of Believe (Belief).

"Due to, and because of, the generosity of our friends and children."

To Believe that there is always hope in our medical field of finding cures and saving our children.

"Is truly God's blessing that gives our children and their families."

The ability to Believe in themselves and to provide a new chance at life over the horizon.

Michael D. Sparks
*Myrtle Beach, SC*

# The Last of the Royal George

Call for the brave
The brave that are no more
All sunk beneath the waves
Just by their native shore.

Eight hundred of the brave
Whose courage well was tried
Had made the vessel heel
And laid her on her side.

A land breeze shook the shrouds
And she was over set
Dawn went the Royal George
With all her crew complete.

Ball for the brave
Brave Kempenfelt is gone
His last sea fight is fought
His work of glory done.

It was not in the battle
No tempest gave the shock
She sprang no fatal leak
She ran upon no rock.

His sword was in its sheath
His fingers held the pen
When Kempenfelt went down
With twice four hundred men.

Elizabeth A. Lewis
*Washington, DC*

## Dear Almighty Father

I have surrendered my will and my
Life into Your healing hands. I have
Also invited You into my heart, mind, and
Soul. I thank You for Jesus, Your blood
And the anointing of Your Holy Spirit.
I pray Thee give unto me Your wisdom
Strength, honor, and integrity.
I thank You for a rejuvenating
Mind, body, and spirit. That I know
Comes only from You God our Father.
I thank You for humility that would place
Me in the likeness of Your son, our
Savior, my Lord in Whose name I can
Ask of You all things and all things
Are possible through Him. A gift of Yours
To me from You in Jesus' name I pray.
Amen

Edward Hadley
*Amairillo, TX*

## Recipe for Emotions

Take two cups of sadness, a tablespoon of anger, and one cup of happiness.  Put a slice of someone you miss and an unhappy event in a bowl of tears, then stir with a spoon until it's ready and has a burst of flavor.  Throw in something you care about, love, or hate, and cook in a crisp oven at 143 degrees until it sizzles with deep feelings.  You can tell it's done when it is drained with tears.  Let it cool until it's moist and sprinkle on a pinch of sorrow.  Cut and serve with a knife and that's the taste of emotions.

Melanie Borreo
*Cliffwood, NJ*

## We are

We are the worth of destiny
    just waiting to be born.
We are the history just waiting
    to be written.
We are the stars of a universe
    not yet conquered.
We are the angels' dust in a
    planet full of expectation.
We are the flowers waiting to
    flourish in full splendor.
We are the unborn and future
    of a dying star in the Milky Way.

Juan Zayas
*Chicago, IL*

## If There Is Never Nothing to Do

If there is never nothing to do start
praying the rosary. Each bead is
Our Father and ten Hail Mary. Just do
it. The joy and peace and feeling
good make the world go around.
Remember every time you hear
a bell ring an angel is being called
to help someone. Pray, open your
mind and bring out the best in
you. For each day is a blessing and
each prayer helps you to be closer
to God. Also living close to
church helps you lose weight because
you have the spirit to do it
for yourself and others.

Carol Turner
*St. John, IN*

I am a seventy-seven-year-old retired college art teacher. After retiring, I have involved
myself with many activities I wasn't able to pursue until then, including writing poetry.
I am currently working on a set of twelve pressed flower collages with corresponding
poems and have a head full of future projects.

## Ode to Battle

On charged the warriors
through the years
Cloaks stained with blood
sweat and tears.
Patriots faithful, tireless
and strong
Challengers, victors, all
their young life long.
Their weapons are mighty
Their footsteps are sure
Our God is their strength
whose commandments
are pure.
Yet God in His greatness
From His mighty throne
is calling again
but now calling them home.
No longer to battle
Their weapons laid down
Come up young soldiers
and pick up your
glory crown.
A dedication of honor
to our American
soldiers of bliss
who fight for the
pursuit of freedom,
religion and happiness.

Emma L. Martinez
*Oxnard, CA*

# Late Afternoon

In late afternoon the sun slides down toward the west
And shadows become long and stretched
As the sun expands in size and its color shifts to red
Before it drops below the earth and time for bed
Bright colors streak the sky and color clouds
As light softens and the day is downward bound.

The heat is reduced as a fog rises from the fields
And a haze moves upward with such eye appeal
And as the haze turns opaque it blocks the view
Of the far off land and fields and houses too
And the late afternoon slips into dusk and dark
As day thus ends and the time of dreams will start.

Philip Grounds
*Vincennes, IN*

# Mother

Memories that will always be cherished within my heart.
Often wondering how my mom accomplished what she did on her own.
Truly praising, and thanking God for giving me such a great mother.
Helping me to be caring, compassionate, appreciative, and grateful for
who I am and what I have.
Encouraging me to do what I wanted and standing by me through thick
and thin.
Realizing that what I've become is in great part because of my wonderful
mother.

Ethel Bachman
*Wrightsville, PA*

# A Day at the Beach

The cold ocean water hits the tips of my feet
While the warm hot sand covers my heels
Red crabs dance on the sandy floor
A baby turtle flipped upside its shell
My family playing in the sand
The dolphins swimming in the waves
While I took a nap on a towel
And I could feel the ocean breeze
while the sun is up high at three
The salty air dried up your mouth
When a gust of sand filled my eyes
And my eyes filled with tears
I looked at the sun set behind the ocean

Lukos J. Buterakos
*Davidson, MI*

# A Retired Nurse Asks

Did I make it better?

Where did all the footsteps
To all the bedsides
Go?
And every door I left
Hoping it was so.

Did all my countless acts
And all the pills and potions
For all their broken bodies
Matter?

All their faces pallor
And all their voices frail
Flutter and swirl to
Dim and distant
Gray and hopeful halls.
Did I make it Better?

So I wonder
And so I must believe
They are in their Heavens
Resting and gone....

And it was Good.

Mitzi Higley
*Destin, FL*

## Sean's Birthday

Thank you, God, for this fine young man, our cherished son.
We watch with pride and so much love, his adolescent struggle
as he emerges from the cocoon of childhood and begins to
know the man he is to become.
The qualities of the endearing little boy have been nurtured to
fruition in a caring young man.
Guide him on his unsure path, for his can sometimes be a
lonely journey.
Above all, let him know how much we love him as we share
the bittersweet growth of boy to man.

Kathleen MacManus
*Bloomfield Hills, MI*

My poem was written at dawn on June 22, 1979, our oldest son's 16th birthday. I arose with my heart filled with thanks for the gift of this wonderful child. I have always loved to write, majoring in journalism at Marquette University. My creative endeavors are given to family and friends on special occasions. Some poems are sentimental while others are humorous. My husband, Michael, and I have been married 46 years and have three wonderful children and four beautiful grandchildren.

# Death to the Devonshires

Look to the horizon boy, right above the mire
The dark and dying day escaping through the fire
One day that will be you and I, our souls fleeing to the end
Out into the Cosmos, with neither enemy nor friend

One day we will be free from our troubles and our toils
Free from this life of sin, the black and bubbling oil
But our feet rest here now, upon these feudal lands
And upon the morrows wake we will make our final stand

Raise the pitchfork high boy, above your bleeding brow
And let those bastards know: "We want our freedom now!"
Sweat escapes the palms as the moment now is dire
We will feast on Tyrant's blood, death to the Devonshires!

Today blood has spilled for the sustenance of land
And so again and again, cycles the tragedy of man
On the land I writhe, pierced by the noble's steel
And so the dying day, melts the hopelessness I feel

Look to the horizon boy right above the mire
The dark and dying day escaping through the fire
Today I feel my soul, fleeing to the end
Out into the Cosmos, with neither enemy nor friend.

Korey Johnson
*Burlington, VT*

## War Casualty

His gentle heart she wounded
with a sigh.
She did love him, but he'd left her
standing idly by.

A kiss, a ring, a letter
now and then
Were all he'd left to bind their love
till he returned again.

But these, themselves were
precious treasures—
Treasures she put aside
for a moment's sensual pleasures.

Too late she saw the chain that
bound them had been broken,
and the words of love her heart now forms
can never be spoken.

Marthall S. Jackson
*Douglasville, GA*

## Clarence

You may be gone,
You may not be gone,
I didn't have anything to say,
Here you lay,
I wish I could have told you,
That I love you,
Farewell Clarence,
Farewell Clarence,
You will always be in my heart,
I will always remember your trust.
I will never forget you,
Never ever forget you,
Thanks for being there,
You will never be far or near from here,
I'll pray for you,
I'll pray for you,
My heart is gloomy,
I don't know why,
You had to go,
You had to go.
Farewell Clarence,
Farewell Clarence,
I love you,
Everyone loves you,
We love you,
We love you,
Goodbye forever,
Goodbye forever.

Lindsay Lindow
*Fairland, IN*

## Snow

Snow
Snow of powder,
Covers the ground,
Pure whiteness,
Pure peace.
The sun peeks out,
Its rays pour down,
Down,
Down,
Its heat melts the snow,
It transforms into tears,
That trickle to the ground.
The snow disappears,
The earth can be seen,
It's as if the snow
were
never
there
at
all.

Ashley Bultman
*Winston-Salem, NC*

# Wrapping Presents

He measures out the paper
Without waste or indecision.
He miters the corners
With mechanical precision.

Then he hands this perfect package
To me to add the trim.
I use some bows, a bird, a rose—
Whatever suits my whim.

If one of us should ever stray
Or take another mate,
Who would wrap my packages,
Or who, his, decorate?

Sherry L. McManus
*Bellevue, WA*

## It Was Me

I saw a newborn baby with its gentle smile and soft skin
Without a care in the world.
It was me.
I saw a small girl learning to walk and talk.
It was me.
I saw a young girl learning to drive and going on her first date.
It was me.
I saw a young woman giving birth for the first time—what a sight to see.
It was me.
I saw a young woman swinging her child under a tree.
It was me.
I saw a young woman going through sorrow and pain of a divorce.
It was me.
I saw a young woman who learned to hold her head up high and face the
world with faith.
It was me.
I looked into a mirror and saw a small frame woman with white in her
hair and much wiser than she should be.
It was me.

Betty J. Morris
*Barnwell, SC*

# Untitled

I see the wrinkles upon my face
It looks a lot like Irish lace
Less hair on my head, but more on my body
My physical stamina has gotten so shoddy
My toenails are thicker, I tend more to bicker
Gave up my bad habits, even the liquor
New moles on my face are sprouting hair
My eyebrows seem to face everywhere
The gray in my hair is growing so fast
Can't remember it being red in the past
Where the hair in my nose came from, I don't know
Never knew bowels could move so slow
Eating prunes every day, sloughing calluses away
The gas is more painful than I care to say
Blue veins in my skin have come to the top
Liver spots on my hands have a new crop
I have to wear glasses to improve my sight
My teeth of course, come out at night
I go to bed early, but that doesn't matter,
I'm up several times to empty my bladder
All things considered I'm just glad to be
And so very happy that you're older than me

Russi W. Arden
*Livonia, MI*

# Loving Lindsey

When God made blessings, He saved one for me.
How would I know how beautiful she would be.
She would make me laugh, and she would make me cry.
She would fill my heart with her big brown eyes.
She would make me thankful as I said my prayer
That God would send an angel and put her in our care.
We thought it would be hard to raise a Down Syndrome child,
But the blessings we've received you can see in her eyes.
Oh, thank you, Lord Jesus, for this grandchild you gave,
Only you know the difference she's made.
I praise you for her laughter. I praise you for her love.
I praise you for the gift that came from Heaven above.
I know I'm the lucky one for the blessing you have sent.
Her name is Lindsey Brooke, and for our family she was meant.

Sherry Horton
*Moulton, AL*

I live on a farm in Moulton, Alabama. We raise cattle and have chicken houses. We have four children and six grandchildren. My first grandchild was born almost ten years ago. We were shocked when she was born with Down Syndrome. We knew very little about it and did not know what the future would hold for her and for us. We would have never imagined the blessings we would receive from Lindsey's life and the joy she would bring us. Lindsey is just Lindsey and we wouldn't have her any other way.

## Falling Down

Fall...
It's the season where the leaves turn brown,
Red, gold, then fall to the ground,
It's what happens when gravity gets you down,
As you spin around and around
Fall,
It's what happens at life's end...
Can't wait to see what's around the bend.
Fall, fall, I love the fall,
And when it's time when life must fall,
This is what I say to all:
Fall,
Fall...
Fall.

Amanda Seifert
*Milford, OH*

## The Note

Forgive me
Oh my peccadilloes,
I am sorry.
Love yah!
Farewell.

Rudolf D. Munro
*Chicago, IL*

Mr. Munro has been a student and practitioner of meditation for over twenty-five years. He runs drama workshops and seminars and is a frequent radio guest on the subject.

## A Round Tuit

Of all Love and Consideration,
We need a round tuit.
Of aspiration and dreams.
We need a round tuit.
Of plans and sympathies.
We need a round tuit.
Of memories and virtues.
We need a round tuit.
Of being humble and giving.
We need a round tuit.
Of being Christ-like and believing.
We need a round tuit.
Have you been a round tuit today?

George Marston
*Santa Maria, CA*

# One Source

Rays of light glimmering surround
Cascading glowing beams of brilliancy
Gleaming fiery glitters of sparkles
Penetrating shadows of darkness and doubt
Vibrating, piercing radiating from Him
The living One, absolute and
Complete source of all power.

Jacqueline Corkery
*Phoenix, AZ*

# The Joint

The Joint is a real place
Unlike any other place we know.
No home, church, school, or club
Can adequately be compared to it.
People refer to it by many names:
The Big House, Motel Hell, Prison, Jail;
The occupants that reside there come and go on a daily basis,
Just as people do who live out in the public,
Except they just don't have the same freedom.
But believe it or not, our thoughts
Can be as strong as any of our institutions;
So could it be that maybe by definition
That the joint is really just in our minds?

Tommy Jammer
*Sweeny, TX*

# Snowy

Winter is very bright,
With snow that is white.

You see white all around,
And bells making sound.

The sound of the bells,
As the little kid yells.

Around the holiday,
People laugh and play.

They enjoy their family and friends,
Some people hope it never, never ends!

Richard Boyd
*Rome, NY*

# Untitled

I had stolen downstairs to witness the last ruby red sapphires
Glow and fall silent in the hearth slowly they dimmed, gradually fading
away
But alas I said to myself why such a beauty and pleasure be stifled
Torn up tissue paper and scrunched up newspapers these forlorn and
tragic tools
Would be all that would rekindle my sweet fire
So it could once again flood the hearth with its warm glow
With the lighter in my hand I set to work to start anew
But the first try failed smoldering to ashes
The second, the third, fourth, and fifth
Moaning in despair my heart ached to save the little burning vision of
hope
Finally on the last attempt a flicker . . . a flame . . . a fire!
I rejoiced feeling happy and fulfilled a weight lifted off my shoulders
I lay and watched as a new mother watches her child
Simultaneously feeding nurturing it keeping it alive
And it was a child dancing on the ashes of old
It was life, it was new, it was hope that burned inside of me—hope
Late into the night my head drooped and my eyes shut and my body
slowed . . .
I awoke early in the morning lying by the hearth—back to reality
To hurt and anguish to sorrow and despair
Questions were thrown at my face all I could do was smile to myself
And say barely above a whisper—hope
For there is always hope for those who believe
Always a radiant light at the end of the tunnel
Always an unawaring flame in the endless darkness

Olivia O'Connor
*Marshfield Hills, MA*

# On Office Productivity

If you work in an office, I think you will agree,
We have a major problem with our productivity.
The problem's universal, the solution is unknown.
When the gals head for the ladies room, they never go alone.

And yes, the march begins at dawn and seems to never end.
What the heck goes on in there is a mystery to us men.
The poor boss stands and tears his hair, he's simply torn with grief.
The day's production goes to pot when the girls go on relief.

It happens every morning and we see it just at noon.
A double file of females bound for the ladies room.
Perhaps the trip is long and rough, the hallway dark and lonely.
Two by two they march away to the room marked "ladies only."

At two o'clock each afternoon, the march begins once more.
And then again at three o'clock and once again at four.
The thing that puzzles all the guys and gives the boss gray hairs,
Is when the gals head for the ladies room, they always go in pairs.

Our CEO is worried so he asked his chief I.E.,
Tell me, sir what can we do for productivity?
The only thing that he can see to make production boom,
Is move this whole damn office down to the ladies room.

Jett Black
*Auburn, AL*

# My Darling Son

Losing my life once again
As your birthday comes around
Every year I feel worse
Not knowing why you're gone

My young son
I miss your smile
I miss hearing Mommy, I love you
My darling son

Although time passes by
Pain is still a reminder
Oh, my dear son
I am crying inside

As my life goes on
One day we'll be together again
Pain no longer a reminder
For my love we'll be together

Julie Studnicky
*North Creek, NY*

This poem was written for Mary Lou Cole, a friend of our family who lost her son. So to all who have lost, I hope this poem helps in some way.

## Crazy About You

I must have been crazy about you.
Why else would I have let you get away with so
Much before getting fed up?
I know I must have been crazy about you.
You beat me up and then you beat me
Down. Fortunately you never knocked me out.
You see, I am still standing. I did not have to
Take so much but I did and . . . I did.

And now you stand there in front of me crying
Crocodile tears but those big crocodile tears will
Never, ever match the ones I cried for years.
I must have been stone crazy about you.
I lost so much of what I had. I lost my friends, I lost
Weight, I lost money and I even lost my dreams.
Yeah, I lost dreams of you and I living well
Together and loving each other forever.

When you came into my life I thought
You were exactly who God wanted for me.
I loved you, cared for you, cried for you and
Almost died for you.

But either you could not or just would not love
Me the way I need to be loved. If you had just
Really loved me, like you promised, we would
Not be here in this mess. You know exactly what
I mean, so please don't call me crazy because I
Am no longer crazy about anything, which now includes you.

Edward Massey
*Wilmington, DE*

I am a former high school math teacher. I was married but my wife is deceased. I have five sons and one daughter. I tutor math for students who want to become Delaware certified instructors. I was inspired to write this poem by one of my students. She shared her story with me. She was going through a very painful divorce and she often talked about this with me after her tutoring sessions. This poem is not just about what was happening to my student. It describes what happens to many people who have finally broken away from a difficult marriage or love relationship.

## Attic Things

Old trunks of treasures
Dusty rooms with unswept floors.
Tattered books of poetry
Bound with love from days of yore.
Old and faded wedding gowns
Top hats, tails, and canes.
Bits and pieces of time past
Just a few old attic things.

A box of old love letters
Tied with ribbons, aged with rust.
A pillow stained with teardrops,
Old lace curtains,
Smells of musk.
Pictures of a handsome couple
A box containing wedding bands.
Memories of a life gone by.
Now labeled
"Attic things."

Mary C. Madden
*Alger, MI*

# Untitled

This spring is like a young woman,
Lush with new rich green growth,
She sparkles with lights
Reflected from the sun.

Eleanor M. Gardali
*Ardmore, OK*

The leaves in bunches rose and fell as the wind fluffed them. Trees glistened as the sun touched their arms. It was a warm, fresh promising spring day. I happily walked by on the road next to a pond.

# Shock

I dreamt I saw two birds flying high,
One by one, they knocked down two stately reeds, as they
swooped out the sky,
I awakened to see the date on the clock
It was 9/11

Jeanette Dowdell
*Ridge, NY*

## Circle of Hope

There's a circle of hope pushing through a circle
Of tears that spans the globe and calms our fears.

Evil and Good walk this world.
Still, kindness expands and smiles unfurl.

When you take a stand to ease someone's pain,
Hope arrives like a warm summer rain.

Open your arms to a feeling called Love.
It flutters in our hearts like the wings of a dove.

Robert D. Margolin
*Westhills, CA*

Big Jim whose company built the fence around ground zero to protect all the brave Americans and Jillian the trainer from the Biggest Loser television show are just a few of over twelve thousand people that Grandmaster Robert David Margolin has helped lead better lives in his twenty-eight years of dedicated teaching. Without one vacation he has worked twenty-four hours a day and seven days a week to teach, train, and then write all night. After spending three years writing his epic martial arts screenplay titled, "Scorch," he turned on his TV and watched a special on Oprah Winfreys's Leadership academy. With tears in his eyes he wrote this inspired poem.

## Ungrateful Love

Why can't you open your eyes
And see how I truly feel inside
My heart is torn into tiny millions of pieces
But this time it won't heal for these reasons
You said you love me, but you don't have any clue
What love means
Now that you gone, you're always in my dreams
How stupid can I be,
For truly believing you that you loved me
You lied, now I'm heartbroken
Words just left unspoken
Didn't even say why
Didn't even bother saying goodbye
How could you find me so easy to forget
You just left me feeling so upset with regrets
It's like you see me sad, but you don't realize the pain
Why you have to be so vain
I'm trying so hard to hold back my tears
Wishing in my mind you would disappear
Hating you wasn't something I wanted to do,
But what can I say, you made me look like a fool
I don't want to see you no more, your words are fake
Being with you was a stupid mistake!

Clarissa Rivera
*New York, NY*

# Hi & Bye

I looked out the window and what did I see,
Tiny little ants as busy as can be.
They were running north, south, and west.
There stopping to greet each other was the best,
Just enough time to say hi and bye.
Back to work is why,
The ants keep busy and work for the Queen.
There is no time for dilly-dallying in between!

Ardel Orphal and Barbara Mulert
*Phoenix, AZ*

While recovering from surgery my southern sister and I (Barbara Mulert) watched these ants at work. We then came up with this poem. Therefore, we would both like to be attached to this poem. We are the "Southern Sisters."Awful21@aol.com.

## Miss Rosa

We called her, Miss Rosa, she feed us when hungry
Clothe us when naked.  A lady of honor, a lady of substance.
She gave us food when hungry, free rent, free water and
A place to live until death.
Truly a lady of honor. A lady of substance.

Miss Rosa calmed the crying children. Smiled
As she rode past in her big, blue 1956 Cadillac.
She showed us love. Gave presents during Christmas
Easter, Thanksgiving and all special days.
Truly a lady of honor. A lady of substance.

We called her Miss Rosa. She showed us the twinkling
Lights on Christmas trees that we had never seen before.
Miss Rosa gave us our first stuffed animal, candy canes and
A red wagon. A kind lady, gentle lady.
A lady of honor and a lady of substance.

We called her Miss Rosa. When Father fought Mommie, she was there
Disastrous fires. Homes burned. She was there.
She loved, showed compassion, she understood. We'll
Give thanks for her presence each and every day.
Miss Rosa; a lady of honor and a lady of substance.

Death will never diminish her worth.
Death will never diminish her love for the unfortunate
Death cannot heal the sadness. For, I still remember.
I exist today because of Miss Rosa.

Sherman Langston
*New York, NY*

## A Father's Love

Have you ever seen a grown up man weep,
For the loss of a son.
He came to me as a gift of life,
And left like the setting sun.

This boy a man so big and tall,
Yet so young.
He loved to live and lived to love,
A life that had only begun.

Dreams to a boy are so real,
Like toys in the sand.
A life to live all fun and games,
To be taken by no man.

How I miss my beloved son,
For part of me died that day.
Until we meet in Heaven's land,
I'll miss you in a special way.

Francis A. Bertrand
*Highgate Springs, VT*

# Till We Part

Last night as I watched you sleeping
After years had taken toll,
Came a fear to overwhelm me,
And lay heavy on my soul.
It was then I thought I'd lose you,
After all these years had past,
As I knew that life was fragile,
And this dream would never last.
So I gently bent to whisper,
In your sleeping muted ear,
To let you know just how I felt,
Though I knew you did not hear.

Please don't leave me in the winter
When the nights are cold and long
I would ever be so lonely,
When your love and warmth are gone.

Stay when fragrant purple clusters
Of the lilacs fill the air
And the artists with their brushes
Paint the landscape everywhere

In the summer I will need you,
When the warmth melts cares away
And the golden sands soothe aching hearts,
While we watch the world at play.

Please don't go when the leaves are red
And the pine is in the air
And the gusty winds paint rosy cheeks,
While we laugh thru tangled hair.

But if you should ever leave me,
I know just what I would do.
I'd gather up my broken heart
And search the earth for you.

Dorris Aguirre
*Far Rockaway, NY*

# I Sit and Rock Alone

Just yesterday it seems, my children
played upon the floor,
and I wiped countless fingerprints
from the windowpane and door.
I kissed away a thousand tears
and darned sock after sock;
and tried to keep pace with the hands
that raced around the clock.
And often when at end of day,
too tired to sleep, in bed I lay,
to think how nice when, children grown
my time again should be my own.

So now I sit and rock alone,
my hands at rest, the work all done,
no little tots upon the floor,
no fingerprints upon the door.
No sock to mend, bruises to kiss,
ah me, how could I know I'd miss
the very things I grudged to do
when I was young, and sturdy, too.
Dear God, if only there might be
Someone again who needed me.

Arthur B. Flaven
*East Bridgewater, MA*

# Hazel

I cry with the bullfrogs like a
small child.  I grow with the daisies,
pretty and wild.  I run with the
horses in pastures so green.  Like
these eyes of mine.
This is me.
The taste of rosewater and rain on
my tongue, a life free with youth
has just begun.  Brown hair that
blows in the summer wind, the
sunset glows on my ivory skin.
This is me.
I climb upon the mountaintop and
fly amongst the land.  One day I'll
swim the sparkling sea, dancing
on a stretch of sand.
I'll live a life of faith and love
and hear my child's laughter.
I'll dream a real fairytale and
live happily ever after.
This is me.

Nora A. Kellogg
*Payson, AZ*

## Wind

The wind is such a miraculous thing
When it moves through the trees it seems to sing
Except on a cold and wintery day
Then the wind acts in a special way
In the winter it seems to howl
Wind puts on quite a scowl
We don't mind it though because soon
Wind will certainly change its tune
Now it will move gently through the trees
Just like a new and springtime breeze
In summer wind is hot and dry
As it moves across a sunny sky
But in the fall it brings the rain
To sprinkle upon our domain
From all of this we can only reason
Wind is changing with the seasons.

Linda Watson
*Utica, NE*

# A Response to Footprints

The man awoke.  He remembered the words the Lord had spoken, "My precious child, I would never leave you at times of trial.  It was then that I
carried you."

The man was confused.  Why hadn't he noticed that the Lord was carrying him?  Why had he felt forsaken?  He knelt down to pray and God answered this way;

"You didn't notice that I held you above danger, said the Lord, because you continued to open your arms to others in their times of need."
THANK YOU, LORD.

"You didn't notice that I lifted your cross, said the Lord, as you were sharing the cross of your fellow neighbor."
THANK YOU, LORD.

"You didn't notice that I held your "time" in my Hands, said the Lord, because you made "time" for me in your daily prayers."
THANK YOU, LORD.

"You didn't notice that I cleared your pathway, said the Lord, because you were following in my footsteps."
THANK YOU, LORD.

"You didn't notice that you kept your Faith, said the Lord, because you always accepted what was to be each day."
THANK YOU, LORD.

"You didn't notice that you shared your love, said the Lord, because you gave of your love freely to others when needed."
THANK YOU, LORD.

"You didn't notice, said the Lord, but I did." Now go in Peace."

THANK YOU, LORD.  The man did.

Loretta Welk-Jung
*Jamestown, ND*

61

# Grayland

I glide a gain to Grayland,
Resting and testing where
Black nor white nor rainbows grow
As glow birds circle while warriors stand down
So shades of gray swirl around,
Spiral up, then go to ground
Bringing me focus on singing wings
Where issues dance while reason rings,
As pouring rain lights Grayland jewels,
For resting and testing where reason rules.

Denny Mason
*Warren, PA*

# A Manifestation of Fallen Dreams

Falling, fallen…to collide with the earth.
The majesty of the skies is diminished.
Mighty wings folded, worthless and still.
Flightless, inert.
Never to soar through the heavens again.
Earthbound forevermore.
How did it come to this?
And yet…
Something stirs in the heart.
A calling to the sky
The will to fly.

Ellen Laird
*Ames, IA*

# New York, the Big Apple

Loud banging music, jammed busy streets.
Welcome to the city that never sleeps.
Wintertime freezing, summertime heat,
Homeless guy wrapped in a newspaper sheet.

Dirty train stations, infested rats,
Folks dancing on subways for change in their hats.
The smell of sweat and urine stays for a while,
Metro cards swiping, jumping turn style.

Expensive stores wealthy girls adore.
Coach, Prada, Gucci and so much more.
Top class guys that dress and talk funny,
Don't go in those stores if you have no money.

Wall Street--busy workers in a rush,
Tourists riding the double-decker bus.
Pushing and shoving without saying pardon.
Knicks getting blown out at Madison Square Garden.

Freezing outside, snow up to your knee,
Just to admire a huge lighted tree.
Rain, hail, snow, sleet,
You can hardly feel your feet.

Taste the Big Apple,
Where all the love seeps.
Welcome to the city
That never ever sleeps.

Brianna Ellis
*Rosedale, NY*

# Ode to Mimi

First there were six, now there are three,
We have another break in the Family Tree.
Oh! Woe is me, what can I do?
The world is not the same…without you.

Looking back over time
I had to dig deep to remember the early years…
Kids, diapers and lots of tears.

We had some fun times and rough times, too,
Sticking together was the thing to do.
Families are forever, that's the way it should be…
Bumps in the road can crack the family tree.

We have lost our Mimi, never to be replaced…
She's in Heaven now, she's in God's grace.
Goodbye my darling sis, I miss you so…
I'll see you in Heaven, when it's time to go.

So save a place for me in Heaven above…
We will all be together…to continue our LOVE!

Teresa C. McCoy
*Irvine, CA*

# The Littlest Tree

People mulling around looking for that perfect tree.
There's a nice one, oh, that's for me.

But in a corner practically out of sight,
Was the littlest tree.
He felt daunted, and so unwanted.

Please look at me, and see the tree I could be.
I can fit anywhere, a tabletop, a sitting chair.

With bobbles hanging
And tinsel strung around my branches,
I'll be a festive little tree,
Won't you take a chance?

But nary a one could see him at all.
We want one that's big and tall, or else no tree at all.

So people came and cleared the lot,
But for the littlest tree, they forgot.

Oh, Mister!
Will you donate that little tree
For the children's ward #3?
To give them happiness and cheer
For getting well this year.

And all the children gathered about
Sing and laughing, and one gave a shout!
Yeah! For the littlest tree that shines so bright.
Like the star that brought Jesus that night.

The littlest tree looked above,
For now he knew he was loved.

Viv Laramore
*Great Falls, MT*

## Good Old Summertime

Summer is here and the pretty flowers are in bloom!
You can count on seeing beautiful birds
and hearing them sing real soon!
The winter winds have blown away,
We are enjoying some beautiful sunny days!
Summer in south is a wonderful season,
We can think of so many great reasons!
The beach is calling, come sun, surf, or swim,
Build sandcastles, throw Frisbees,
or pick up shells if that is your whim!
When we think of summer we remember the Fourth of July,
that great Independence Day.
There are so many ways to celebrate and here are several ways:
Picnics, barbecues, beaches, and sack races,
Watermelon after picnics, and all take their places!
You look up in the sky on a hot summer day!
Pretty hot air balloons are soaring up, up and away!
Let's count our blessings, give thanks to the good Lord and say,
You don't need a lot of reasons or rhymes
To enjoy the good old summertime!
Have a great summer.

Dorothy Riggins
*Tamarac, FL*

## Bill

There once was a guy named Bill
who had plenty of money in his till
and then one day he got married
and neither of them tarried
to seek out the land of bliss
beyond New Jersey's mist

Bill's wife was a nurse
who never carried a purse
and then one day Bill's pocket read empty
and she still wanted more than plenty

So a return trip was in order
until they reached the border
and their car ran out of gas
and all she could say was alas
we've had a blast
that didn't last

Perhaps one day
along his way
he'll meet his old hitchhiking honey
with plenty of money
that's still searching for the land of bliss
beyond New Jersey's mist

George Ondish
*Great Meadows, NJ*

# An Interior Poem

The wall is plastered with wallpaper
filled with a sea of flaming red roses
with lemon colored berries and
olive green leaves
tucked between them
forming giant birds
that dance in a frozen pattern
across a pale beige wall that
surrounds an array of
dusty cardboard boxes
stuffed with
dingy wrinkled
clothes that give off
a wild smell that
engulfs the room
A soft light from
a small dust covered red lamp
highlights the rumpled bed covers and
the saliva stained pillow
lying on the floor next to
a pink feathered bedroom slipper
Near the door lay
the other slipper
Its soft feathers
scattered about

Mary L. Smith
*Columbia, SC*

# An Old Man's Hands

I looked upon those tired old hands, soon ready for the grave.
Once they were young, once they were strong, and once they were so
brave.
What have they done, those tired old hands, through all their many
years?
Some years were glad, some full of joy, but some were full of tears.

A combat aircraft once they flew, 'gainst tyrants cross the sea,
they fought a long and bloody war, to keep our country free.
Risked life itself in days gone by, like all those boys who flew,
many young hands were stilled for you way up there in the blue.

They fought the fight with all their might, and some went down in
flames.
Their glory and their sacrifice our country's flag proclaims.
The cheering crowd they saluted proud on fourth day of July,
the marching veterans that they led, heroes parading by.

One day a pretty girl they held who soon became a bride.
They struggled through life's stormy seas with her right by their side.
Then soon a newborn babe they held as fathers' hands all do,
with hopes and reams and wishes for mankind reborn anew.

Oft times those hands together clasped, in fervent, silent prayer,
to ask the Lord's forgiveness and plead for the Savior's care.
Those tired old hands will soon pass on, as mortal hands must do,
to join their God, the Lord of all with others tried and true.

Whose hands are they, those tired old hands?
Those tired old hands—are mine.

James Sauers
*Hurricane, UT*

69

## God and Goddess

Please hear my plea and prayer
Please accept my plea and prayer,
We've been separated/incarcerated and financially stressed
We've been given all kinds of tests
What we request is a YES, please release us from all of our stress
Please send us a surprise, an angel in disguise,
Who will handle all financial stress and separation/incarceration
situations
Please bring my son out of jail with the speed of light
Please give me monies, so my pockets won't be so tight
We've tried everything in our powers, so our prayers would
successfully reach the Positive Power.
So my Son and I do not have to rejoice under the roof of a
correctional facility
Please make our plea and prayers a reality not a probability
Please no more tests
Just say YES GOD AND GODDESS

Eunice White
*Far Rockaway, NY*

# Mom

I feel loved when you hold me in your arms
My heart grows as big as the moon
I feel like child on Christmas morning

You look in my eyes and whisper I love you
I do the same
I love getting your warm gentle hugs
That lets me know how you love me

I will cherish our love forever
I love the feeling when you gently kiss my cheek
It feels like a beautiful angel fluttering her wings on my cheek

When I am feeling down you are there to hold my hand up high
You are my mom I only get one
And you are the one I love most of all
The love between us will never fade

Your eyes as shiny as new diamonds
You are a beautiful creation
You are locked in my chamber of love forever
You led me through the darkness and into the light

I know I don't tell you enough but I love you
I love you so much I would do anything to keep you by my side

I love you
And don't forget it
You are the only thing I can't live without
Mom, I love you

Kyle Barth
*Clarkston, MI*

## Teenage Girls

It's funny how a teenage girl's mind works
Some call us loud, pleasant but some think we're jerks
So, as a teenage girl, let me tell you how our life usually goes
How we try to be something else, or in other words, how we pose.

Make up, hair, beauty, and clothes
The four most important things that a young teen knows
Eyeliner, mascara, blush, and following trends
Oh believe me, that isn't where this poem ends.

Going out with boys is more important too
How they look, dress and especially who
But if you're a little heavy, not pretty enough, or like me, too tall
Get used to the fact that most guys don't give your personality a chance
at all.

You might not look attractive but maybe you do
Us girls with our big mouths will talk about you
Whether we mean it, or the green monster decides to come out
Rumors are spread, there's no doubt

We may act independent, but magazines like Teen Vogue are where we
get most trends from
I think we should be ourselves, unique, or who we want to be. It's as if
our minds are numb.
When I see people acting like something they're not, it makes me want
to hurl
It seems we all have to look just like the twin of Cosmo Girl.

Though we can be tough, we also can have the best of times
Hurting my friends would be like committing so many crimes
We have sleepovers, go to parties, and can usually be found at the mall
Wherever we are, my friends and I have a ball.

Nicole Kosoff
*Woodland Hills, CA*

I am a fourteen year old girl who lives in Southern California. I love to play volleyball, go
to the beach, swim, draw, go out with my friends, and write. I wrote this poem at thirteen
because as soon as I hit the teenager stage I noticed how many things had changed since
elementary school. I noticed how different girls had become, how interested in ourselves
we sometimes were, and how mean we could be. This inspired me and by remembering
past events that occurred and things about girls I couldn't understand, I was able to write
this poem.

## Feelings of a Kind

Sometimes I feel like rubber
When I'm stretched beyond my means
Sometimes I feel like tin
All rusty and just rattling around
Sometimes I feel like steel
Unbendable, unbreakable and extremely strong
Sometimes I feel like plastic
Capable of being molded into some wonderful form
But most of all, I like to feel like a diamond
All brilliant, bright and loved by everyone!

Carroll DeWitt
*La Grange, KY*

## You're My One and Only Sweetheart

You're my one and only sweetheart
You're my one and only love.
You're the only one that I ever told
That you're the one I love.
I remember that day we met,
You said you loved me so.
You loved me much more than this world,
But now you let me go.
My darling, please forgive me, and please come back to me.
You're my one and only sweetheart
The only girl for me!

Michael F. Matushin, Sr.
*Palm Bay, FL*

## The Other Man

The other man and I would talk about
How our lives were torn.
How in our lives we have to seek out
shelter from the storm.

One day we were alone and then
He kissed me and he said
"Let's make love instead."

So I took him to our bed
A bed already stained
with joy and tears.
I let go of all my fears.

Then I changed the sheets
and I changed my mind.
I hung the blankets on the line.

I changed the sheets and exchanged my soul.
And though you're all I ever wanted,
all I ever planned to hold,
the other man who loved me
is the thing that made me whole.

Julie Baker Marby
*New Smyrna Beach, FL*

# Who Am I?

Do all the answers lie inside me? for I am the one that is in need…
It seems like every step, move or route I take puts a different path in
front of me…
I don't know what to do there for I don't know what to think, or even
what to say, questions always remaining in that useful piece of flesh
called the brain and lingering feelings still remain in that tiny, but most
powerful place called the heart.
Who am I? I don't even know… what lies inside me, in front of me, in
the back of me…
Who is this human I call me? Like the person who carried me for 9
months told me I am just trying to find myself, but what is the word,
"Myself?"
What does it mean? Does it mean, the characteristics that make up the
word "Me"… is it the choices a person makes that makes up their lives…
or is it the feelings they feel and the opinion they have for everything in
life? I want to know who I am.
Is it because of me if my life is hard and dreary, or when my life is
content and joyful?
I just want to know. For I am the one who chooses the paths I walk in.
Even though God is the one that published the chapters of my life I
am the one that follows through them. I can't keep living my life not
knowing, "Me."
Why? Because I am the starter of my own dreams and not just only that,
but the starter of my own downfalls and the starter of my own being.
So I don't need anyone else to tell me who I am, just me, but because
God is the holder of my life, He is the one that guides me in the right
direction on helping me find me… so I ask once again, "Who am I?"
And now I should know because God made me a human being…He
made me to make mistake, to help, and to learn… to just be me.
But that question that I ask myself everyday still remains, "Who am I?"
Who is "Myself"…Who is "Me?"

Micahh Scott
*Detroit, MI*

## Poem for Me

Through the frost
Alas a thought,
Time spent years past
We talked.
Distance over sea and air,
To wonder and wander
How proud you are,
Or can you be?
Sing out in joy
The day will come
Live in my eyes
I dream for you.
Whisper softly,
Smile, laughs
One day I hope
You will be
Two lives now three
A wish un-touched
But in a dream.

Diana Richardson
*Yonkers, NY*

## Separation

You loved him, he loved you he never wanted to go…separation
it hurts he was special he wanted the best for you it was dark and stormy
you find on the wall written in blood I'm coming for him you didn't pay
attention you thought it was a joke
…separation
You come home to man holding you ransom your guy dies to let you free
unharmed…you cry you have nothing to say except I hate myself I'm
stupid I should have paid attention to the wall
…separation
You loved him and he loved you find a new guy but its not the same you
turn around and commit suicide because you want to be with him
…separation
You are no longer
You are with him somewhere in the land of the dead
Being welcomed by the death band
Together
Forever

Ashley Haeseker
*West Babylon, NY*

## Dear Daddy, Please Don't Go, Stay Watch Me Grow

Dear Mommy, I thank you for keeping in a special place to grow.
Your nourished me, you loved me, before my face could show.
Now I've arrived, after 9 months to wait.
You and Daddy showering me with love, protecting me from hate.
I love you both and your warm soft touch.
However, this poem is to tell Daddy, when he leaves, I miss him so much.
Dear Daddy, I want you to know, I feel you kiss my forehead before you go.
Mommy says you have to work to provide, I wish I could sneak in your pocket.
I'd go along for the ride!
Dear Daddy, I wish you didn't have to go.
I want you to play with me, laugh with me, watch me grow.
I am thankful that I'm your son and you're my dad.
I feel so loved when I hear you tell mommy;
"I'm the best of anything and everything you ever had!"
Dear Daddy, I'm too little right now, I can't wait until I'm one or two.
Then I can finally show my love and wrap my arms around you.
Dear Daddy, in just a few months I'll be able to crawl.
Will you play games with me like blocks and chase the ball?
Dear Daddy, I miss you, but don't worry, Mommy takes good care of me all day.
I just can't wait to see you open that door, with that smile that says, "Lets Play!"
Dear Mommy, don't be sad, I love the both of you.
However, if I could talk, I would tell Daddy to stay home with me, too.
Dear Daddy, Please don't go!
Stay home, watch me grow…

Dawn Parilla
*Circleville, OH*

78

## Bittersweet

Without love
No pain
Without you
No Joy
Josias
Mirror to the soul
Your eyes are mine
Little Mouse
Heart bigger than body
Forgive me!
God's Gift
A non-existent childhood
I lived mine through you
I grieve the loss of yours
Identity Theft
You cannot be if you never existed
Blue-eyed, blonde non-entity
Just ask Mom!

Joan DeLuca
*Bronx, NY*

## Running

Wind blows. Leaves float...I run.
Reeds yellow. Air chills...I run.
Fires crackle. Plants fade...I run.
Sleet falls. People shop...I run.
Youngsters skate. Sleds swoosh...I run.
Rains arrive. Buds burst...I run.
Cows low. Tractors drone...I run.
Kittens nurse. Babies gurgle...I run.
Sun shines. Forests flourish...I run.
Dogs bark. Squirrels scamper...I run.
Lawnmowers rumble. People laugh...I run.
Sol rises. Earth rotates.
Seasons change,
Life continues and still I run.
I miss you.

Susan Gehris
*Walnutport, PA*

# In My Room

The candlelight burns, my bedroom turns, into a holding cell
I haven't forgot, and my optimism rots, where all my ideas dwell
It's dripping, slowly, dripping, past the tipping point, I'm tripping
Into thoughts I haven't brought myself to think in quite some time
As my hand turns to twitching, and my drink I still sit sipping,
As I soak in all my substances, and sulk in what I've got
I seek not what I shouldn't have, to have a stable life
But my loves alas, are all but gone, and they always say I have done
them wrong
so I sit alone and sing my songs, to the girls I could have had
it's never them and always me, just because I do not like myself
these walls that make my holding cell surround my brain and make my
hell
I cannot speak and I cannot tell just when it all will end
So I fan my flame, and pass the blame, and make up rules to play my
Game
I blame the system and people of fame, and everyone who shouts my
Name
In anger, hatred, disgust and disdain
I sit alone inside my room, and dread the day when the morning looms
All because I know I am doomed, to repeat the same mistakes

Adrian Lyons
*Antioch, CA*

It seems to me, that although it may be far too much to ask the world to fully accept
one's actions completely, and too much to even attempt to understand why anyone would
ever do anything, it is not too much, in my opinion to ask of the world to keep an open
mind. My writing is not me, and will never define my constant existence, it is rather an
extension of a thought—a snap shot of my head at only one point in time. Forevermore,
but never less.

81

# I Do Have a Life

I may be that homeless child
Walking the streets
I may be that someone behind
The prison walls—accused wrong
Praying to be free—
I could be that person out in the cold
I might be that someone in a nursing home
growing old—
I just want to be someone
And I am
From an all-time athlete
To a service person serving their country
A mother holding her first child
in arms.
All these and more want to stay
away from harm.
Wherever life takes me—it was
meant to be—but I am
someone—and I do have a life.

Kay Todd
*Minoa, NY*

# A Corner without Light

A dark corner
Black as night
You look outside,
Yet see no light
The wind whispers your name
Calling you to the ocean's waves
You pray for peace
Yet get nothing but a cold shoulder in return
You would rather rot in hell
And let your soul burn
Spitting flames all over the place
Erase those memories
Erase that face
Pale moonlight in the window
You see that face wherever you go
Run, run away
You cannot escape it
You must face the pain.

Adriana Levine
*Los Angeles, CA*

Love is the essential nectar of life. As an aspiring writer, I am enchanted with the beauty of words and intrigued by the art of language. Difficulties I encountered throughout my life have motivated and inspired me to write poetry. My poetry is a cesspool of conflicting emotions, longing, passion, experiences of unrequited love, and the pain of true love. My inability to forget someone is reflected deeply in my poetry and is my profoundest inspiration. I write because I still love him and miss him. So live, love, and laugh. It's all you need.

# And Even So, We Shall Rise!

Hearts heavy, eyes filled with tears
America's soul cries.
Death has claimed thousands by terror through the skies
Spirits low, families and friends mourn
A nation says its goodbyes,
To heroes slain...
And even so, WE SHALL RISE!
Powerful symbols destroyed, homes and jobs lost
America's mind tries
To remember peace and security
As hate and love collide.
Fearful children, trust and innocence raped
A country unifies.
We share pain,
And even so, WE SHALL RISE!
Pride thrives, faith in democracy lives
America's flag flies
From the mountains to the valleys
Every city far and wide
Heads high bringing life to the pledge
We memorize,
We're crimson stained,
And even so, WE SHALL RISE!
Through the tears, through the sadness,
America replies,
United we stand! We shall overcome!
We'll never compromise!
We'll pray to God for guidance and for grace
For He is wise,
And stand for justice for the world
Wherever hate reigns,
And even so, WE SHALL RISE!

Joan Hagans
*Brooklyn, NY*

I was inspired to write this poem after the events on September 11, 2001. An event which could have easily broken our spirits, only brought us closer together; I believe the poem chronicles the event from the emotional standpoint. As New Yorker, my husband, three children, and I had never been more proud. As our country continues to learn, grow and break barriers, we're even more proud to be Americans. Let us remember, always the importance of family and unity. All my love to my husband Chris, my daughter Joavan, and my sons Joshua and Eric. ~Peace~

# The Living Room

ceiling darkened by dust and age,
pasted walls with antique paper,
dignifies floor's matted trail.
photo's past memories hang from
assigned rustic pointed tacks.
years of talk, sleep, and play
sag rundown blue sofa and easy chair.
grandfather clock, cornered, coffin shaped,
ticks away grandfather's time.
stick-like rocking chair, lined up
for surfing mindless TV programs,
commercials and pleas for money.
bookcase stocked with "Wisdom of the ages"
as nearby outdated telephone remains silent
and replaced by modern cell.
French doors seal old sewing room
while kitchen gateway becomes
meal time smell of gruel.
empty rooms past time like
darken cemetery's tombs and vaults.
clock's pendulum memorizes
tired patriarch while ceiling fan
turns in haunting silence.

Robert A. Pence
*Valparaiso, IN*

# A Whisper

As former president Bush
stood in front of the stairs to Air Force 1,
and said goobye to Michelle Obama,
I saw his lips move and say to her
"I promise you."
When they hugged farewell
What was the first part of that sentence?
The part that was whispered in her ear.

I will be in touch; I promise you?
You will be great; I promise you?
It will be okay; I promise you?

He was sincere.
He looked her straight in the eyes.
What exactly did he promise?

Cheryl S. G. Podob
*Easton, CT*

I was mesmerized by the events of the inauguration. It was a momentous day in American history. The feeling of pride in America's journey for the pursuit of freedom and equality lives strongly as it did when our forefathers signed the declaration of independence. What extraordinary men they were. Look what seed they planted and in turn created. I live in Easton, CT and have been writing poetry since I was in 8th grade. I share my life with my husband, our 2 daughters, our puppy Ben, our guinea pig Sunshine, and lots of family and friends.

## Monster Serum

Monster serum runs through my spine
causing devastation in my life
Monster serum cannot be held
as we are left to wonder, what the hell
Monster serum has no limits
takes on humans with a vengeance
Whom to wonder if there's hope
especially left immobile by no choice

Vanessa Gomez
*San Diego, CA*


## Love of War

Is love, not love, but love of war,
To kill, hate and separate,
To fight for what they think is right,
But not to know for sure,
To send loved ones off to war,
We pray for them forever more,
To wage war—a hostile force,
Can something tell me, what's it all for?
Fighting, killing and destroying God's land.
I feel in my heart, this is not God's plan.
How much longer can we be fooled.
You think it's time for " Prayer back in school?!"

Chauncey McCummings
*Washington, DC*

## My Brother

I know you went away one day,
But you didn't say goodbye to me
It just wasn't the way to leave,
I know when God called you had to go
Did you give up or was it just your time to go?
I still look for you from time to time.
But I pray and hope you are with God.
I hope you are looking down on me
Smiling in your own special way.
I know you just went home to rest,
I look forward to seeing you again someday.

Josie B. Hall
*Park Forest, IL*

I am a retired school district employee. I worked twenty-three years at the same school district. I always love to write poetry. I was inspired to write this poem because my brother passed away a few years ago. So this is in memory of him. I just wanted him to know that I miss him and I am still thinking of him always!

## Was and Am

I was young and ugly
Her voice led to acceptance
I was blinded by an untold world
Her loving hand gave me eyes to harmony and chaos

I waited for nine long years to find
My guardian and teacher, mother and sweetheart
I needed someone to teach
My love would listen to understand what no one could

I wanted to save her from her blood
She was a warrior against a universe of corruption and hate
I melted in her arm because I could not help
She kept me by her side instead of leaving like the rest

I hoped for my best friend's heart
She gave a silent opportunity that invisibly came
I was too naïve to feel my skin torn instead of the tumor
She found an idiot, a reject of genetics
He is my nemesis

I watch so carefully, hopeful through teen years
They fight like tortured monsters, and are plotted on to split
I keep her close, despite the demons and the stars in my head.
My love will linger like the kiss I should've gave
I will always be in love with my Amanda, hoping we can be.
Maybe, maybe, maybe?

Nick Dukauskas
*Scranton, PA*

My name, or should I say other name, is Torsten V. You may wonder where my inspiration comes from. I hate reality usually, but "Was and Am" is the most beauty I could get from reality. I believe poetry and writing should stay pure and clear. Before this, I'm a high school senior and a writer working on my first book, "Pinstriker." Movies are my inspiration, whether "Batman" or "The Hills Have Eyes," these stories have taught me everything I know. So, all harmonies, and you may hear from me again.

# Do You Remember?

Do you remember the true meaning of Christmas?
Or to that question do you have to pause?
Has Christ's birth for Man's salvation been substituted
by Old Santa Clause?
Are your hands folded in reverence
and your knees bent down in prayer?
Or are your stockings hung by the chimney with care,
in hopes that Old Saint Nick will soon be there?
Do you remember the story of the three wise men
who came from afar?
Who were guided to a tiny stable
and were led by a bright shining star.
Have you gone to visit the little babe who was born long ago,
and laid in a manger?
Or has his identity eluded you
and he yet remains a stranger?
Is your time so preoccupied in buying presents,
that you forgot about God's greatest gift of love?
That He gave His only begotten Son to mankind,
sent from the heavens above.
So this Christmas let us reflect on the true meaning,
as we go about our daily living.
That this day is Christ's birthday,
and remember this season is the season for giving.

Willie E. Rushing
*Chicago, IL*

# Love Me Enough

I just want somebody to love me enough to keep the tears
from falling; to keep the hurt from coming. I want
somebody to love me enough to change me… To free me. I
want somebody to love me enough that they open their eyes
and see me. I want somebody to love me enough to blur the
lines that separate us, so much so that we appear as one. I
want somebody to love me enough, to remind me that
every part of me is alive. A love so strong that if any pain slips in,
loves causes it to subside. I want somebody to love me
from the inside out, to love me from the outside in. I don't
want to be able to begin to understand where that love
starts. I don't want to be able to fathom that it will ever
end. I want somebody to love me so much that their touch
feels like heaven and their kiss like bliss. I want somebody to love me
into believing that love actually exists.

Patricia J. Wynn
*Los Angeles, CA*

# Not Trying 2 B Noticed

I'm the type of person who likes to look ahead
Never looking back into the life that was misled
Misled by the media, peer pressure, the whole scene
Caused to struggle with maintaining my Christianity
Asked God to open my eyes so that I can see
All the devil's tricks that were being cast upon me
Knew God created me with purpose
All my hidden talent would now head 2 the surface
My mission statement I'll sit in my room and write
Putting my thoughts on paper… it just don't come out right
Asked God to send it to me in a vision or a dream
So that all my potential would be seen
Creativity, personality, growth, Chanel that's all you
Now that I have all these characteristics what am I supposed to do?
Not let people get to me with all the needs of confrontation
Set myself aside because I'm a chosen generation
I'm living my Christian life strong, willing and focused
I'm not gonna put myself out there, I'm not trying to be noticed!

Renee Smith
*Bronx, NY*

## Within this Sorrow

When a loved one leaves us,
We find ourselves left in the dust,
We cherish the moments shared,
In hopes our loved one knew we cared.

Our lives are forever changed,
Plans re-arranged,
We ask ourselves why the loss?
And the moment seems to pause,
But no words come,
For we are too numb.

Our grief runs high,
For this devastating loss cannot be denied,
Our hearts torn,
We wonder how we can go on.

But what of our loved one's missed tomorrows?
We can only nod our heads in sorrow,
But within this sorrow we'll soon find,
The love our loved one left behind.

For those of us here,
Never fear,
Our loved one will always be near,
In our hearts and in our minds,
From now until the end of time.

Sau K. Tam
*Silver Spring, MD*

# First

Your first is something special
A new experience
Marks a chapter
In your life

First meeting
First date
First "I love you"
First time holding hands

First kiss
First breath of life
First St. Valentines Day
First love notes

First gift of love
First picture together
First moment
First year

These moments are of love
A pure of heart
Love that last forever
An immortal bond

Michael Madain
*Allentown, PA*

## Paradise

Palm trees swaying in balmy breezes,
bouquets of fragrance from the isles
dancing merrily along the shore.
Star-filled night, sky has retreated,
sun is shining, rays are glistening
on dewdrops of early morn.
Children laugh, ever happy,
building castles in the sand.
Hawaii is calling you.
Dreamy days at the beaches,
hidden along palm-lined paths
unfound treasures will delight.
Hawaii's gentle arms await you
beckoning, waiting to embrace.
At last, you have returned.

Lisa L. Johnson
*Lynnwood, WA*

# Yes We Can

Who would have thought that I of all people would not have the back nor
trust or be a believer,
one of our own, educated, hard worker, family-orientated, an achiever.
My heart full of distrust and pain from firsthand experience and what has
been,
not honorable, too many single mothers, divorce, war, jail, corruption;
few thoughts by women
of men.
Not sure how to think or feel, since all my people have never been
thought of in a good way,
our words, behaviors, skin tones, whether working, not working, in
school, not in school—being judged day by day.
Now the document that said it was written for all seems really true,
and I can stand up and be proud of both anthems believing in the red,
white and blue.
As I think of the many activists that walked this path, the tears began to
fall,
but I know, it is because of them that I am—we all are able to walk and
stand tall.
I now have a sense of proudness and joy for a country that fairness
wasn't to be seen,
today and always, those who fought for justice are a true example that
there is no "I" in team.
To me, the evils of the world have been fought, and for once, the good
has won the race,
with love in your heart for all, the higher being on your side—you will
always come in first place!
I am now a believer and I know the top of the mountain is for all-to-be,
and that everyone is equal and has a right to freedom and Li-ber-ty.

Ilana L. Eakels
*Chicago, IL*

When people meet me they think she isn't being real, that it's an act. Why? Because of
the love in my heart and my creator that I lead my life by who I believe created us all. I
wrote this poem because people like me or any person with skin tone are judged unfairly
everyday and equal rights are unrealistic. But I hear a man who speaks exactly how I
believe and now people like me are finally in the spotlight. Righteousness has prevailed.
Let freedom reign!

# My Life as a Yooper

I was born in the '40s.
In a small U.P. town
When life was so simple
And the world not so "down."

My parents worked hard,
For what little they had
In a two-bedroom bungalow,
Four children, Mom and Dad

Our bedrooms were so cold,
We could see our breath in bed
As a small burning wood stove
Barely heated the front shed

We had no real plumbing
Just an outhouse, pump and pantry
Mom heated water on the wood stove
For our dishes, baths and laundry

Our first TV came when I was twelve
No color, one channel, one movie per day
Then came a phone, with a party line
No VCR, no cell phones, no credit to pay.

We lived off the land, and happy we were,
With gardens, and wildlife, and fishing galore.
My parents worked hard with the tools they had,
But if they'd look down from Heaven, the world they'd abhor!

Nancy M. Fitzpatrick
*Waterford, MI*

# The Life That Was Given

At first the sound is like a slow gentle gallop of a horse.
As I listen I discern the distinct sound of a cluster of leaves as they are
blown across the pavement.
I stare as they continue on their path with no plan and no destination.
The leaves had a time to bloom and now a time to fall.
How beautiful the process of dying can be.
Without life the leaves would never have bloomed into lovely green
canopies that provided life and protection for just a time.
All life lasts a season and endures many moments of sunshine and also
many moments of turmoil and uncertainty.
The life is given and the promise is made that you will experience your
one season.
The length and the prosperity of the one season are in the hand of the
Giver.
The Giver knows the beauty of each life and the amount of time it will
bloom.
Enjoy the season as you enter each phase, both the beginning and the
end.
Every creation will one day return to the giver, may it be with a joyous
heart and true thankfulness for the gift that was received.
The life that was given.

Laura Suckow
*Norwalk, IA*

# Dear Midwest

Dear Midwest, You've done your best
Providing food, and clothes and rest.
It breaks my heart to have to go—
But go I will when I see snow.

I love thy amber waves of grain.
I love thy many fruited plaines.
But when a snowflake begins to fall,
I love Florida most of all.

Your lake so wide, your buildings high,
Your Magnificent Mile where I buy, buy, buy.
But when Rudolph's nose beings to glow
I'll pack my bags and off I'll go.

I'll miss Shakespeare, Wyndella, too.
Of course, I will miss all of you—
Daley, George and Blagojevich
I'm flying south like that wicked witch.

I wish you happy winter days.
I'll think of you in many ways.
But lying on the sand so warm
I do not have to fight the storm.

I'll watch a cloud traverse the blue
and, Dear Midwest, I'll think of you.
But when the temperatures begin to soar
You'll find me back at my own front door.

Marilyn Kessler
*Crown Point, IN*

# Borders

Death walks the land,
My brown eyes can see him.
Through the nights these questions flood my people—
They hear it sigh; I see the heart of the night and I too, question
existence—
In search of Eden I cross borders.
Why do you hunt me brother?
Ancient blood unites us, and you betray me for what?
Am I a reminder of whom you killed?
I can forgive, can you?
Search your heart, try and answer the questions that form a pool around
You
I see the coming out of your eyes.
Maybe
You're crossing borders now and
Am I on the other side?
Do you see me wearing your eyes?
Does death walk your land; do you look at him?
Do you know his eyes are empty and offer no rest?
Does he search for you, is that why you tremble?
I have just begun, and now must cross borders not seen by mortal eyes
I must search for answers where my existence ends and
Fire is transcendence—
I must carry this flame to depths of human soul,
To look for my people buried within time, underneath skin and bone—
I crossed borders in search of Eden—

Larry M. Reyes
*Harlingen, TX*

My home is closely located to the Mexican-American border, that we really don't think
of as a border. I am a second generation Mexican-American, who has lived here all my
life. What inspired my poem is this closeness to the border I mentioned. Perhaps to
reveal a truth or perspective on how a non-existent thing affects people and their lives in
such a profound way. I wanted to capture the re-birth one feels as the crossing threshold
of a border, any border for they're all around the world and perhaps the guilt one feels
when the forsaken haunt our dreams. A promise of a new world and opportunities the
silent sacrifices that echo through this country.

## Tragic Moments in Time

Without knowing value tragedy abounds
Sad affairs grow resistant to response
Pointless fears play with our thoughts
Restrictive glances and heartless laws

Arms embracing with empty or heavy hearts
Created in dreams unable to suffice reality
Such tragedy when un-manifested love lay idle
Passed by unnoticed in a preoccupation with ourselves

Passions long lost desires turned to dust
Dispassionate lies dealt out so as not to harm
Opposing any questions that may be debated
Held captive by revolving conversations with oneself

Bundled between the comfort of the linen of our beds
Vacant eyes scanning the ceiling for esoteric visions of hope
Tragic boredom that brings tears due to pathetic absentee emotions
Feeling heaven perhaps only when someone has been born or died

Longing for the luster in the twinkle of the eyes of our sons and
daughters
Who have all grown and moved away and we are left with silence
Angry with my own companionship I roar back with dark accusations
Barely able to talk or walk I lay motionless…dead

Yes, I'm sure now for nobody was there to be recognized as my own
And my spirit spoke to me quietly; "Where is my Love now?"
"Can you not see with your vision, my dear? I heard and then felt the
void float away
And all those that I had challenged to love in life were there beside me
too, forever to stay.

Wendy L. Buckingham
*Aurora, CO*

Writing poetry releases me from fear, regret and disappointment. I let these distractions explain themselves on paper until their own words are exposed for what they are: Illusions. In silence I am answered with heaven's voice clearing the way to transcend the madness of it all. The voice of reason releases me from the darkness into the light. Poetry is abstract and appears unclear but it is unrestricted and naturally flows like a flower that one day lived and in the next has died only to our eyes' view. It's all beautiful as Hope Springs eternal.

# Our God of Love!

I was walking down the shady lane
All peaceful and serene
When I heard a voice within me say
"your life is blessed as it can be!"
"your health is good, your family's fine
with wealth and happiness to share!"

It's time to rest and say a Prayer
For peace and health for all who care;
To set free the troubled soul, the lonely
one, the ill in need of Prayer.

The God above is a God of Love—Love for you and me!
Just ask in faith and He will hear
He is always near! His answers clear!
Your dreams will be what are best for you!

God is Love for one and all—large or small
Wherever you may be! He asks
Us to share His Love with those who are near,
Whose cries we hear and help along their way.
To bring peace and cheer for all our years with prayers
to Him each day!

Jessie C. Maurer
*Tempe, AZ*

## The Broadway Lights

Why are we here?
Why do we perform?
For the Loved Ones who've
perished…
And the return to The Norm.

Each performance is a dedication
And, you our friends and
Audience—
Are our inspiration.

For, we form a bond
To show they've not
Died in Vain—
This is our way of fighting-
To assuage the Pain.

As artists and audience
We are united in our cause…
To show the importance of peace—
And the horror of Wars.

So do come and join us—
Be Proud—Be Aware—
We're performing each night
For our Friends Who
Are no longer There…

Jackie Lyons
*Long Beach, NY*

# Musings

I love the Christmas season, the sights, the sounds, the smells
Of gingerbread and roasted 'Tom', the tinkling of the bells
The little children's laughter, anticipation keen
And softly falling snowflakes in every wintry scene.

The horses and the buggies in days of long ago
Would pause before the opera house and disembark below
And then through double doors so wide and up the several stairs
The ladies and the gents would climb and leave behind their cares

They'd reach the auditorium, prepared to see the show
And note the gas lights on the stage with twinklings all aglow
An aura of excitement would be noticed in the air
As umbrellas were planted below each creaky chair

There was a place for ladies' hats, so lovely and sedate
And each would get so comfy, prepared to celebrate
"A Christmas Carol" by Dickens as music filled the air
The rafters rang as patrons sang and joy was everywhere

The opera house still stands today with life a swifter pace
"The show goes on" in this grand Hall with trap doors still in place
The wooden floors are squeaking now, the seats are rather thin
But when the curtain opens up, the show will still begin

And so this Christmas season our Little Town of Lights
Still glows with pride as folks turn out to witness all the sights
And folks stop in the opera house to dream of long ago
When horse and buggy transported our patrons through the snow

Irene Gidley
*Cedarville, OH*

## Tact

Washing words in a basin frothy with laundry soap
I grab the words in my reddened hands and scrub them hard
Working out the grime and grit
Until they are clean enough
For you

Alane Brown
*Durango, CO*


## Time

Time moves across the land without
a backward glance and counts each
day that takes its ease upon our
windowsills, salutes the sun's parade
above the earth, then watches
evening's purpled sky fade into dawn.

And we, in turn, surrender to this
emptiness which offers nothing
in its name but years, yet dazzles
with a sensuous beat that drives
us, reeling, from the arms that
rocked us once upon a time.

Lucy E. Finnigan
*Honolulu, HI*

## My Uncle Wally

My Uncle Wally used to tell us things
Not with words but with red sore eyes
Rambling drunken dreams run wild
Often dream not even available just wild
He let his life be dominated by missed opportunities
Left in a glass in some dingy bar lingering smell of cheap perfume
An empty bottle turning brain cells to liquid
Less of him standing in his love of lies
Lost days deleted
Making what was left of life manageable
The bottle always leaking the top lost to mice
My Uncle Wally laughed vociferously
Throwing his head back, punk sanguine redness in his cheeks
The body telling on him wanton now bent inward
He was a welder sticking steal to steal
Unable to mend the slush that now were his thoughts

Dianne W. Corder
*Eden Prairie, MN*

# A Prayer for Strength

Shall my dark turn into light for it has been gloomy and I have found
nothing but sorrow, hate and strain. And that very night sin was we in I
was sin Oh LORD, Oh LORD!  Help me begin again.
Shall my shadow turn to bright, let thee faith, and hope keep me in your
presence for I will not deceive or leave thou place that was
granted to me.
Shall my evil turn to love for I desire to be fed with heaven's
prosperity from up above grab my hand and pull me out the malicious
and viscious world that traps me from seeing the light.
Shall my story move the dis-believer's soul may the devil no longer
brag and boast of his false riches and my presence for I will not let
temptation keep me, I refuse to reap thee karma that follows me I
rebuke thou cruel demon that wishes to bring me to my knees
Shall my angels surround me and my light of belief blind the devil as
he reaches to mark me, NO NO NOW HE CANNOT SEE!  But my
GOD has saved me, yes he saved me so powerfully it's his grace that is
within me I deny it no longer for now I am stronger.
Shall no man shut the door to my glory that has been open by my
LORD, and I will BELIVE in BELIVE in BELIEVE!  No matter  the
circumstance with the devil I will not dance but let the LORD pass
through the city of despair
in I dare any man to doubt his works because the LORD has and will
keep me through my rise and fall so here I am standing proud and tall
knowing that the love of GOD brought me through it all

Mariyah Burton
*Las Vegas, NV*

# She Was Paris

She was Paris
Before Hilton
All blonde and blue
With pink and gold highlights
A Venus De Milo with arms
And a Mona Lisa smile
Ripe as a summer peach
Her paparazzi was
The Varsity Football Team

Hearts beat faster when near her
Mystery was her friend
Her secrets could never be captured
Her secrets could never be captured
The adventure was the trying
She was sunlight
Here today
Gone tonight
She was Paris
Before Hilton

Arthur Baggot
*Denville, NJ*

## Antagony

I cried my face red, my heart disrupted
With what they were imposing on her
This little flower, Therese, so innocent, silent and guileless
prisoner of body and bed.
Powerless against the screaming mouths for justice,
misspent and twisted.
Sending her to her death for just being who she was.
How she was their ears closed, their minds made up
She is of no use. She must die.
Thou shall not kill, He said in gentle loving breath
What you do to the least of them is also done to Me.
He hung His head while sacred tears rolled on the parched earth
The sadness, for this Jewel the silent one with big brown searching eyes
Her temple in disrepair, her heart bursting with
all the flurry round her bed
Lying eyes with blackness in the soul of he who shared
her bed so many years ago.
And yet some eyes with love and caring strained and hurt and in futility
also silent spoke of their love for her, her earthly family standing by
their hands tied with the will of conscienceless cold unfeeling men
Law in black appropriateness, dour and disobedient heartless laws of
Men and not of He who made them, and they who doled them out
with icy carelessness, meanness unbending
"She does not suffer" they blatantly proclaim. How do they know? Has
anyone returned to tell them of their false veracity???
So my wish for all of you who crushed the little Flower is this
And when the day for your ETERNITY arrives, and it will
you know and you stand knocking at God's gate
Then my wish for you is that your gatekeeper be forever deaf

Rose M. Campbell
*Spring Hill, FL*

# How the Typical Barbie Doll "Covers Up" What Lies Below

First she spends an hour on her undoubtedly flawless hair.
This balances out what is lacking below it regarding the true
meaning of beauty that just isn't, and never will be there.

The she puts on her makeup to "cover up" all the ugliness that lurks
below her conceited surface and all that remains.
Don't forget the white strips she sticks on her teeth to clean up
the vile insults that exit her mouth, which had to have left some
stains.

Now on comes the push-up bra to give a "boost" to her already enlarged
self-esteem.
Then to take the attention away from her bloated ego she adds the
tight and revealing clothing.  Are you starting to see what I mean?

On we go to her extra high heels to look down on her companions that
she
felt were less worthy from the start.
How dare we forget her pricey nails!  A necessity to look glamorous
while "picking " her equals apart.

To top it off she adds her expensive jewelry to her body to the
cheap personality she displays.
Last but not least she sprays on her overly strong perfume to
bury the stench of the trash that lies beneath her commercial ways.

I wish she would realize that beauty is only skin deep, because
it's what's on the inside that makes a person unique from all the
rest.
I guess she sadly will never learn that though because
she lives in a superficial world where only her looks can
subside her distress.

Best of wishes my dear…from the bottom of my heart!

Stephanie Nuttall
*Lebanon, PA*

## A Girl Once Known

Here I sit outside myself, begging to get in.
Watching, waiting for some hope, but all appear so dim.
I see the tears roll down my face, and part of me breaking down.
My legs collapse from underneath, but yet there is no sound.
I do not hear a single thing; I cannot bear the pain.
The screeching silence all around, it happens once again.
Let me in! Let me in! Bring me back inside!
Surely if I am out here, some part inside has died.
Never will come back to me, a haunting, empty place.
I cannot reach the girl inside; I can no longer see her face.
Where did she go? This girl I knew, I thought she was okay.
Just a lie it seems to be, everything appears so gray.
Darker, darker as I go, I can see inside her soul.
A fiery place, an empty space, the truth we'll never know.

Sarah Miller
*Richmond, VT*

# Maple Syrup

In the woods so calm and peaceful
In between the maple trees
Collecting the sap in the morning
The cold is biting at your nose
Cold nights and warm days
Make for the best sapping delight
Boiling the sap all night
Forty gallons of maple syrup
So sweet and sugary
On your pancakes in the morning

Brady Lollman
*Hamilton, NY*

# Counsel

Once upon a time in distant past
A Cherokee chief was sitting with grandson
Chewing on buffalo fat
The boy had broken tribal rules
Wanted to know why and what to do
We have two wolves inside us said the chief
One is good, the other a creep
Both need obedience
Which one wins? asked the boy
Of this inner puzzle
The one we feed, exclaimed the chief
Therein lies the struggle

John W. Albritton
*Summerfield, FL*

## Space

Space…an everlasting thing
Are there other life forms out there,
Or only in our imaginations?
Could we but someday travel to distant planets?
Arriving in the "New World" the way our ancestors did coming to
America.

Valerie K. Hackbarth
*Evergreen, CO*

## For Just a Moment

I remember a time…
When only you were on my mind…
Never though I would find…
A better friend

Time carries on …
And feelings fade away…
Here we are today…
Staring at the sun…

Where … where do we go?
Where do we go from here?
Or do we just continue to stare?

Águeda López
*Brooklyn, NY*

# Dream

I see you there
Feel your hands upon my face
Your arms around me
Your breath upon my cheek…light as lace

I feel your skin
Smooth as silk, and just as nice
I smell that scent
That from the first it did entice

I sense your strength
And to hear your voice
Sends shivers down my spine
No, they are not by choice

I hug you and lay
My head on your chest
Relishing the warmth you give
Yes…I like this best

You kiss me
A simple gesture, and yet
So filled with love it was
I'll never dare forget

A siren blasts in the distance
I lash out in panic
Crack open an eye…5 a.m. Monday
Oh…Fantastic

Jenna Kelty
*Conifer, CO*

## America Standing Together

Although this tragedy will be in our minds forever, we will overcome it
by standing together.
America stand tall with pride, let's wipe our tears and bring out the
strength that
we have inside.
Terrorists can run and try to hide, our nation will make them pay for all
the innocent who died.
Men and women of honor you are loved and missed, all a part of
democracy's long
sad list.
We all need to pitch in and do our part, give money, give blood, work
hard, that's a start.
Americans dig deep inside, we all have to be ready for a very long ride.
People of the world there was an attack on freedom, but rest assured the
perpetrators will be brought to trial for everyone to see them.
For now our flag sits at half-mast, but when the flag goes up and the
rubble is clear,
everything will be back to normal or so it will appear.
Let us remember we put our loved ones to rest, we will not become
complacent again, instead we will be ready for the next test.
I love my country and as I write this I cry, I'll do anything for my people,
even go to
war and die!

Roy Vincent
*Barstow, CA*

# Time with You

Sometimes I sit and quietly ponder about our time together...
It seems it was too quickly over, changing like the weather...
We laughed at times at silly things, cracked jokes about the news...
We climbed some hills, slid down a few and cried a tear or two...
We disagreed on one side, then readily agreed upon the other...
Yet through it all we lent support and gave to one another...
We marveled at the setting sun, held hands in the glow of the moon...
Never dreaming for a moment the end was nearing soon...
These days we had together were but our space in time...
Creating special memories that were only yours and mine...
We shared a bunch of good time and weathered through some bad...
But now we've hit the final chapter, the one that leaves us sad...
For one of us must go, the other has to stay...
Fate has made the judgment call and now it's time to pay...
The thing I want and ask for most is dignity left intact...
I wish to pass on over, holding hands with you in fact...
He promises eternal life to all who will receive...
His gift of dying love for those who do believe...
So don't put me in a box and leave me where it matters not...
For being close to you is what it's been about...
Now the sand is speeding swiftly from my earthly form...
Please take me in your loving arms and hold me while I'm warm...
Weep not for me my darling, for this is not the total end...
My spirit waits and watches, and time again with you I'll spend...

Julia Lyons
*Jeffersonville, IN*

I've been told I'm a spitfire and that's probably true. At sixty-eight years young, I am the mother of four and stepmother of three. I'm a grandmother of twenty and great grandmother of seven. I need to see the brighter side of things. However during the writing of this poem I lost my oldest son, Happy, in an accident and my youngest sister to cancer. I am a breast cancer survivor and my husband of twenty-two years has had a quadruple bypass. Poetry has become my lifeline, I love to put our life and happenings in to verse.

## Living Remotely

As I close my eyes to play the movie of my life tonight
Will I replay all that has gone wrong or all that has gone right?
Will I pause at the parts that made me feel happy and over-joyed?
Or rewind to where I thought that my heart was broken and destroyed
Will I fast forward to my favorite parts when I lived life without a care?
Or mute out any scary scenes I do not want to hear
Will I want to turn the channel when things weigh heavy on my chest?
Or think about and appreciate how much my life's been blessed
Will I want to turn the volume down when things were loud and crude?
Or turn the knob back up again when I'm in a better mood
Will I adjust the color according to the way I feel?
Or leave it just the way it is and accept it for what is real
Will I always repeat the bad scenes that made me sad but strong
Or look forward to my future and pray that it is long
See I can't erase the commercials or make my life drama-free
I can't take control of life's lessons but I have control of me

Sandra L. Gordon
*Piscataway, NJ*

## There Walks a Woman

There walks a woman I know
She sees talent
A woman of strength
This talent is not hers
A woman of beauty
Could this talent be hers? No

There walks a woman
A woman of gentle kindness
Her family is quite an amazement
A woman of modesty
"Very talented, nothing like me," she would say
If this was a reflection would it show?

There walks a woman
A woman of understanding
We shouldn't always be thinking
But if we didn't, could we come to a conclusion?
A woman of dignity
If there is love will it grow?

Lovely and graceful as a butterfly
Strong and beautiful as a tiger in the night
Someone must tell her as we all know
Look in the mirror
Come on there you go
There walks a woman

Susan Rice
*Wheat Ridge, CO*

# Maybe

Maybe I should start
to let myself fall completely apart.
Into oblivion
out of this world
no love for this girl
who loves completely
yet discretely they slip away
longing for the day I will say
You are free
to leave me be.
So you don't have to wonder
if the best you put asunder.
Because I left you at last
to be another mistake of the past.

Gabrielle T. Peebles
*Denver, CO*

# The Ultimate Sledding Trip

Winter is surely a unique kind of year
Snowflakes fall and blanket the ground,
and outside, children create snowmen like no other.
Families enjoy skating,
and taking a look at the breathtaking beauty.
But nothing will ever compare to the greatest thrill about winter...
Sledding.
Whoosh!  Kids zoom by on their sleds, giggling the whole way down,
flying over bumps of snow, as their scarves flap vigorously behind.
Down, down, down they go,
and as soon as they reach the bottom,
they're back on their feet again, sprinting up the hill.
Each time, every step is repeated,
yet, each time is a new, exciting experience, down the rugged, snowy
hill.
After hours on end of snowing, each child pushes themselves to do one
more run, trudging through the snow, all the way up
From personal experience, the last run is always the best of them all,
the one to top off the sledding trip, to make the good even better.
Tired and whipped, yet filled with happiness after a great day, they all
head back to their cars to head home . . .
and the wind, blowing softly, seems to whisper gently, "See you here
next year."

Nicholas Wodtke
*Shelby Township, MI*

# Lady and the Tramp

One Christmas morn, John dear and Darling got a surprise
It was a little puppy with big brown eyes
They named her Lady
And nine months later they had a baby
John dear and Darling went on a little trip
They left the baby and lady with an old lady with a bad hip
She treated Lady very badly
So she ran away to a back alley
She met a tramp, Butch
And he got her some lunch
They ate spaghetti while the stars twinkled above
Now they realized that they are in love
When Lady came back
She saw a dirty rat
He tried to get into the baby's bed
But Lady smacked him on his head
John dear and Darling is now home
When they walk in they hear terrible moan
They saw a dog they never seen before
Also a rat lying dead on the floor
They let Butch stay
And Lady thought "Horray!"
Now the house is full of laughter
And they lived happily ever after!

Alexandra Hansen
*Newark, DE*

# Not Too Young!

Take my hand,
Come with me,
There's something you need to see.
Hold on tight, here we go!
I'm taking you back to the day I met the man of my dreams.
You say, "There's no way, you're way too young!
You say we don't know what we're getting into,
but in fact we do. You just don't want to see it because once you open
your eyes you'll
no longer see me as a little girl.
Now it's time.
One more time take my hand.
I'm taking you to the day of my wedding where you say,
"I give you my daughter to love and to cherish forever."
At the start you said no way.
But look at us now as the happiest couple around.

Makenzi Uehling
*Afton, IA*

# Waking Nightmares

The copies whirred loudly
I tried to sleep on the overused black leather sofa.
Every fifteen minutes a worker
Dropped coins into the vending machine.
Crunchy bags of snacks hit the metal trough.
I see only the empty
Inside of my eyes.
An eternity later,
A loud click opens the lock on the thick wooden door.
A snack seeker had silenced the television.
Leaving only the buzz of the waiting copiers.
Suddenly, a man's voice.
Even at the age of 8 I knew my step dad
Shouldn't be there
They argued
About us staying in the break-room overnight…
"It was too loud, too dirty, too public…"
All the things he thought our house wasn't.
He spat out a hollow apology
For his blows and her bruises
His empty words vibrated like the copiers
He gave up and left, for now.
We stayed. I still saw only black
Nothingness behind my closed eyes.

Ariel Johnson
*Davenport, FL*

## Luna Moth

I found the world in powered wings
floating on a summer breeze
fluttering like a kite
beautiful
in the night

Close enough in a dream
Angels' wings comfort me

She told me everything
that she would be
so few years, the end is near,

Close enough in a dream
Angels' wings come for me

Luna Moth for a time
you are here and you are mine
Luna wings flying strong
carry dreams all night long

Close enough in a dream
Angels' wings cover me

Luna Moth, for time
you were here and you were mine
Luna wings in the night
far too soon end their flight

Zach Ramsey
*Lake City, SC*

## Silent Place

Do you know that place where everything's still?
A quiet place with only time to kill.
That quiet place where no one can distract your mind.
Quiet, so quiet no sound of any kind.

That place where the water flows and the winds gently blow.
That place where I long to live day and night.
Where the sun comes up and then goes down,
But I won't frown.
That quiet place will still be there to wake up to
Even if the sun turns blue.

Shhh…Listen, while the ocean waves clash together in that beautiful
way.
Where is this silent place you say?
I'll give you the answer right away.
The way to this silent place is the golden arch to your mind
Where silence is yours to find.

Jaelen A. Horton
*Cincinnati, OH*

# Like Two Sumo Wrestlers and an Invisible Locomotive

Poetry comes around like an uncle
who has drunk just enough vodka to tell you
how much he loves you.  If it stays,
you have the Buddha on your porch swing.

Bob Dylan will check in
to your Bed and Breakfast, write
a song about your pear tree and growing old.

You will want to go skinny dipping
but the critics will figure out twelve ways
to put your clothes back on.

Poetry will kiss the soles of your feet, pull down
the power that others have over you.
It will break the egg of the world open,
streaming with thick newborn color.

Nancy Pulley
*Columbus, IN*

## Soldier's Son

A little blonde-haired boy stands at attention, crying at his father's grave
Beside him stands a wounded soldier, the one his father died to save
The flag is folded; the rifles fire; the sound of Taps fills the air
His mother's cries break the silence, she knows the burden she must bear
Back home, times goes on; school begins again
He tries to ignore the whispers and those who stare at him
He does what he can to help his mom: good grades, a part-time job to
help pay bills
But his future is always a sore subject, a battle of wills
"Son, you can be anything you want, why go and leave me?"
"I must follow in my father's footsteps, I'm going to West Point, the
academy"
Four years later his mother is crying, tears of joy and pride
She watches her son graduate, with his new wife by her side
The new battle is one the Army never trained him for
He holds his newborn son while tears run down his cheek and hit the
floor
Several years later he is packing, off to fight a war
"Son, please fill my shoes, take care of your mother and one thing more
Always search your heart to do what you feel is right
Now give me a kiss and a salute, I have to make my flight"
Father disappears into the plane, mother and son a sad goodbye
They watch until his plane is just a dot up in the sky
Letters coming back and forth, each one is a treasure
One day a telegram brings tragedy, not pleasure
A little blonde-haired boy stands at attention crying at his father's grave
Beside him stands a wounded soldier, the one his father died to save

Lesley S. Shirley
*Crystal Lakes, MO*

I have been writing since I could actually put words together. I wrote this poem in
about 3 1/2 minutes. As a former member of the U.S. Air Force, I have strong ties to the
military. My grandfather, father, cousin, husband, son and nephew have all served. I am
married to my husband, Rod, for nineteen years and we have five children named, Chris,
Iain, Deborah, Shae, and Jacob.

# Untitled

We master our ways and world,
We conquer wisdom
And forgive the pain.
Some pray to winds,
Some talk to Lord,
Some simply smile at falling rain…
And just like children we believe we *can*,
We'll be again,
We'll love again.

Ekaterina Nelson
*Tewksbury, MA*

# Kindness

It's kindness when your nice to each other
Even if you don't like one another
It's hard for us to listen
When your friend is the one that glistens
I wish there was a way
I could actually say
What if I become mad
And you became SAD
Will we still be friends
Even till the end
I really want to say
Kindness is the way

Josephine Decker
*Brick, NJ*

# Chains

Ebenezer met his former partner's ghost
And the rattling of his chains were heavy, Because of his burden.
Ebenezer was given a chance to lessen his
Burden, his chains.
Just like we are, but his burden is heavy,
Just like the chains we carry.
It does not matter whether you are guilty or
Not.
We all have our own chains to carry.
Our own burden!

Peter Hernandez
*Visalia, CA*


# My Imagination

When I reach for the gateway that leads to enchantment,
I am pulled toward magical allure and contentment
Where visions dressed in paint drench my imagination,
Allowing each thought to fade into a world of fascination.
Imagination seems to blend my world of reality with dreams
Where diamonds can erupt from glittering sunbeams.
Visions ensue transforming little things
Into dreams that seem to have taken wings.
Imagination enables the discovery of new ideas to form,
A place in the mind where seeds of invention are born.
When mental scenarios and imaginative thoughts capture my mind,
Great rewards of insight I feel destined to find.

Dee Timmons
*Colfax, IN*

129

# What Music Means to Me

Everlasting and echoing,
Without words, it sighs.
Forever and always,
Filling dawn and the nigh.

Unexpected and unexplainable,
To hear is to believe.
Patient and waiting,
With music, all can see.

Close your eyes and listen,
To the music in the air.
Each life so involved,
With music, always there.

A wonder, this communication,
To me, it's all around.
Captivating each moment,
With each and every sound.

Touching every heart.
With everyone it shares,
It is everything and nothing,
the music everywhere.

Marissa Cecil
*Owensboro, KY*

## Two Brothers

Two brothers
Born apart by years
Held together by love
Two brothers
One a gifted learned
One a challenged student
Two brothers
One living for the future
One clinging for today
Two brothers
One a man on Earth
One a boy in Heaven
Two brothers
Connected in spirit
Forever in time

Bryan Reynoso
*Glendale, AZ*

# Jazz Man

Once upon a midnight delight
A sound of might came into flight
Catchy was the jazz man
The graceful sounds out of his trumpet

Laughing at the crowd
Distinctive sounds blew more with gusto
A hurricane of fireworks flang and rang
Doubled insane blame
Legend he became

Never seized to discontinue his flippen' sound
It swing has flinging cats' fond
Jazz they would say with frightful gleam
Never was a jazz man so clean
So jazzman hit fame…

Edward C. Habis
*Manassas, VA*

"Jazz Man," reflects my musical creativity which has been influenced by my upbringing. I grew up in a culturally diverse, multi-lingual, and enriched environment. It was a mix of South American and Mediterranean heritage. I also lived in and visited countries in West Africa, Middle East, Asia, and Europe which exposed me to a diversity of nationalities, cultures, languages, and their music. During the past two years, jazz and ragtime became the focal part of my musical life and in writing and performing my own piano music my imagination led me to write "Jazz Man."

# Life's Journey

As we go through life we have joy and we have sorrow
But whatever happens, we must always look at the morrow
We must be happy to just be alive
And be glad that we can survive
When you left and just went away
I just lived from day to day
But now I have a new love whom I know will be true
So I am sure that I can live without you

Lorraine Kroll
*Chicago, IL*

I started writing poetry in grammar school. Unfortunately, I didn't write anything for several years and then I took it up again. I am so glad I did as I can always think of something to inspire me. It gives me such a feeling of fulfillment. I like to write poems that will give people hope for a better tomorrow.

## Love

Love isn't just a feeling,
But a decision that we make
A commitment and a choice
A journey that we take
Love is the unending thread
that binds two hearts together
An everlasting gift of faith
And the promise of forever
Love is a gift that can only be given
And can never be taken away
A hand to hold, a heart to touch
A memory made each day
Love remembers little moments
That often pass us by
Like the colored leaves of autumn
And a blue December sky
Love is like the wind
you cannot see, but only feel
The presence of its comfort
That lets you know it's real
Love should be held onto
For you should always know
Hold onto love forever
And love will never let you go

Kayla Mirabella
*West Pittsburg, PA*

# When Snow Melts

The cold winter's chill has left the air,
And sparrows are singing without a care.
Tiny pink buds have blossomed on trees,
Waiting to be pollinated by the birds and bees.
Grizzly bears are coming out of hibernation,
And are seeking food without hesitation.
Rain is falling, fresh, from the sky,
As young baby birds spread their wings to fly.
Clouds are rolling by, so gentle and free,
And the flowers have blossomed for all to see.
There is an old poem, I don't know where it's from,
"When snow melts. what does it become?"
It is not a cold, wet material thing,
When snow melts, it becomes spring.

Caitlyn Slavich
*Sunnyvale, CA*

# Renewal

In the neighborhood old people
Moved day to day
Marking time until death
Quietly stole some away.

One by one sad faced houses
Closed against the world becoming
Silent witnesses for those
Who gave them energy and life.

With the quietness of night snow
A new faced generation
Claimed the dying energy
Of the worn places.

The last of the elders smiled
The knowing smiles of the wise
As the rebirth of old places
Brought a glow to their sunsets.

Venora Rodgers
*Pittsford, NY*

I am an African American woman who has been employed by a human service organization in Rochester, NY for over twenty years. I have three adult children and eight grandchildren. Words and language have always been important to me. I can't remember when I did not read and write poetry. My poem "Renewal" was inspired by events and recollections that occurred after my mother had a stroke. The neighborhood was in decline as the senior residents died or moved away. Young families began to move in and reclaim the neighborhood. It was as if this act of renewal gave the remaining elders joy and a feeling that they were leaving a valued legacy.

## Mayflower Pilgrims

I walked today where they had walked so long ago,
I gazed at the land which they did clear and tend and sow.
The echo of their voices I heard within the rooms
Of the Howland House, down where the heather blooms.
The mighty sea that brought them to this favored land,
Is still washing o'er that rocks and beach and sand.
I felt warmth from the sun that shown on them 300 years ago.
And I stood there wondering and wanting to know…
Were they frightened or hungry,
Did they suffer from the cold?
Did they wonder if they should
Have been so bold?
Were their hearts ever sad
And filled with despair?
Did they long for their homes
In England so fair?
As I stood at the places they had lived and worked and been,
I thought how blessed I am to have them for my kin.
When at last in reverence I stood upon old Burial Hill,
They were all around me, their presence I could feel.
I am stronger for having walked in their footsteps today,
And I will try harder to overcome challenges that come my way.

Anita Crokett
*Safford, AZ*

I am eighty-eight years old. Early in my life I gained an interest in genealogy. I discovered that John Howland, who came to America on the Mayflower is an ancestor of mine. Through the years I studied the history of this group of Pilgrims. So I was overjoyed when at last I was able to make the trip to Plymouth, Massachusetts. As I toured the Howland House, visited the replica of the Mayflower, stood on Burial Hill gazing at john Howland's headstone, my heart was touched and I wrote this poem.

# Peas

Beneath the shade of the cherry tree
We sat in the summer shelling peas—
Grandma, Barby, Mom, and me.

How could such a boring task
Be much fun you might ask
As we sat upon the grass?

It was the loving company
That meant so very much to me
As we sat beneath the tree—

Shelling peas and shelling peas
Before the winter's chilling freeze—
Grandma, Barby, Mom and me.

Sally McCarthy
*Olalla, WA*

# Peace

If time stops ticking
If people stop fighting
If we all stop killing, hurting or even punching and kicking
Just take a moment listen read what I'm writing
If there is peace before us
For all that I want
For all that I need
For Peace on Earth
And everyone Succeeds
No War and Gangs
No Criminals in Chains
No Laws or Commands
Throughout all the lands
Everyone just holding hands
No anti-religion no borders
No kings to give orders
Everyone just Equal. No Rank or Stand
Every Race Holding Hands, thoughout all the lands

Kenny Coston
*Wauconda, IL*

# Another Time

Childhood
Horrific yet exhilarating
Constant Bickering
Little Remorse
Sleepless nights
Relaying Messages
The yelling is piercing

Night is my sanctuary
Curiosity is my fuel
Always pondering
Short days, long nights

Life is shifted
Child is rising
Molding someone new
Intellect within grasp
Alternate realities obsolete
Childhood is life

Life is present

Kevin Cole
*Bel Air, MD*

## A March Snow

From my window,
I see trees
decorated in white,
ready for the holidays
long gone.
I've waited
for green, for buds, I should be depressed,
but nature resists me
with her timeless beauty.

Carol D'Lugo
*Shrewsbury, MA*

## Our Country

What's happened to our country?
The one we love so well.
What's happened to our country?
Is it going straight to hell?
God gave up many blessings
in many countless ways,
But greedy politicians and society are leading us astray.
Countless lives are being lossed and debts we have to pay
Because we love this country in many special ways.
God help us find solutions
to solve each daily task.
Each day love one another as if it were our last!

Ilene M. Laswell
*Las Vegas, NV*

141

# A Day of Play

On a day of play,
don't go astray
Work can be done
another day.
Share your time with
those held dear.
There're so few times
throughout the year.
Go play golf, give
it a try.
Or lay on your back
and watch clouds float by.
You could sit by a brook,
dangle a hook.
Hop on a bike or take
a hike.
There are so many things
"one" can do
But it's always more fun,
When it's shared with "you."

If there's at least "Two."

Dennis Hembd
*Kent, WA*

## Grandma's Silent Goodbye

I think about you every night and each and every day
The very time and date of when you passed away.
It was Thursday June 16th at 8 a.m., a call
From Richie telling me that you had left us all.
I didn't know how to react all I felt was pain
My heart broke into pieces, I though I'd go insane.
Laura led me back to see you lay there stiff in bed
I kept saying to myself, "Wow, she's really dead."
Ever since that very day my emotions, no control
The devil, he came up from hell and took away my soul.
Sometimes I cry at night and almost never eat
Sometimes I feel so bad I hardly ever sleep.
You are not forgotten and all the things you did
The times we spent together when I was just a kid.
I wish you were still here with us, like you didn't even die
So I wouldn't always feel so bad and feel the need to cry.
So I guess that's how life is you know, you live and then you die
But before you left I wish you'd said, "I love you and goodbye."

Rebecca A. McCauley
*Columbus, OH*

# Pleasure of Pain

Pleasure is my intellectual mind,
The pain that comes within is destructive.
But once I'm blessed it seems to be a crime,
And the character is always corruptive.

When I look in the mirror all I see are bruises,
Like a car that's been totaled.
And when it rolls down the window all it does is cruise,
So it pumps its gas so it can be local.

Oh pleasure oh pleasure, oh pain oh pain,
The blood that rushed through moves rapid like a plane.
The pleasure of pain needs to be trained,
It has to be slowed down, I might need a cane.

It is the Victim of my Imagination,
Freeze! Boom! Lock it up?
Pleasure of Pain needs rehabilitation,
Now let's go and see if it can be put up.

So what will it choose,
Life or Death?
Does this choice suit you?
It's very complicated like a wreath.

Now you feel ebullient,
Of the craziness
This has made my mind crazed,
Pleasure of Pain.

Lyric Wilkins
*Lithonia, GA*

# Words Aren't Enough

The way you make me feel inside
Compares with nothing else I've known
You were the one who made it clear
My life would not be spent alone
We'd gone through our fair share of pain
And done some things we might regret
But the first time you spoke to me
Was one day we'll never forget

Always dreaming of the future
Not knowing you were waiting there
Feeling I'd reached the very button
You proved someone could truly care
Thinking about you all the time
Almost seemed too good to be true
Could it be I'd fallen in love
With every little thing you'd do?

Words aren't enough for me to say
How far I'd go to hear your voice
We've only got one chance with this
And have already made the choice
While gazing at those hazel eyes
Reaching hands draw each other in
Lost amongst such sweet-scented hair
Feeling your lips caress my skin

Elliot Burrows
*Meadville, PA*

# Untitled

It has always been on my "To Do"
list to write a poem
Memories, subjects and ideas come to
me at work, before bedtime and always when alone at home
When I saw your ad, chuckled and thought yes, this contest is calling me.
Should I go for it? Why not, it's never too late. I hope you agree!

Sylda J. Hutt
*Pembroke Pines, FL*

# A Great Winter

The trees whistle in the wind.
Crisp are the leaves that still cling to the branches.
Frozen is the grass that appears to be standing tall.
Winter comes with falling temperatures and a cold, blowing, wet breeze.
The snow is starting to fill the gray color sky.
The wind wisps the snow past the window as they set by the fire.
Crackling is the flame bright, red and yellow in color.
Children gather at the window waiting for the white blanket of snow.
With winter coats, mittens and sleigh at hand, they frolic in the fluffy
white mixture.
Hours pass as the children play merrily.
Wondering, as they soar down the rolling hill,
Will this great winter last?

Debbie D. Shepherd
*Lima, OH*

146

# My Life!

My life,
is no longer like a ship
tossed aimlessly
helplessly
upon rough sea's and treacherous winds of life.

My life, has a purpose
a destiny
despite many mistakes
a horrid past.

For even in utter darkness
silence broken by deafening cries of anguish
a single beam of light
can change the face of despair to hope.

My life, is no longer my own
for there is One
who calm's the raging storms of life
makes no mistakes
Loves me unconditionally
who guides me with wisdom in the
right directions of life to follow—
Jesus!

Robin Rae
*Franklin, PA*

# Journey's End

I'm just passing through, so please, don't cry for me
It was my time to go, what's meant to be will be
I may have become old, my body tired and worn
Or maybe I came, a beautiful, sweet newborn
I could have been a child, my potential never met
Or maybe in my prime, my wedding date just set
Or maybe I'm a teen, my future still unknown
My parents dreams were crushed, when I went to my heavenly home
I could be your parent, whose life was whisked away
We will meet again, I look forward to that day
I could have been a mother, leaving husband and children behind
Or maybe I'm a father, of the very best kind
I could be your sister, or your brother too
Share to your childhood memories, of people that you knew
Maybe I was your best friend, you told your secrets to
We'd laugh and talk for hours, I shall miss those times too
Your loving wife or husband, whom you held at night
The one you gave your heart to, the one you knew was right
I could be a favorite aunt, who always brought a smile
Or maybe that wonderful uncle, who would sit and talk awhile
Whoever I was to you, whatever part I played
Just know there is a reason, why he left and went away
Our life is a mystery, each day, it is new
So hold on to your faith, it will see you through
So don't grieve too long, give your heart time to mend
For I will meet you one day, at your journey's end.

Allyson B. Stalvey
*Watkinsville, GA*

# Ardor

Gaze down
for underneath the glass is yesterday, tomorrow, and now,
Look deep—beyond the rim—for I know they were there.
Like a fleeting image—love is lost.
Yes! I'll have another—they go down fast—too damn fast.
If only once more I could taste.

Look deep
for in the ripples are my dreams—liquid gold.
Like the ripples, my dreams seem intangible.
I'm reaching—always reaching, but as the ripples fade away,
so do all my hopes and dreams.

Gaze More
for on the surface sits a man-made coldness,
like the one that encases me so.
I've often heard the winds whisper that
the coldness will melt with warmth is presented.
When he does—if it does.
I'll live yesterday, tomorrow, and now.

Look Deeper
for at the bottom, always motionless—like I appear it
it's what they call backwash—
I call it my last wallow.
I look up into the glass I briefly—
turn realize—it's empty...

Gaze Down
for underneath the glass,
I exist yesterday, tomorrow, and now.

Chandra Staton
*Phoenix, AZ*

149

# Bless Him

There is a man among us
His eyes a hue of brown
Demeanor of shear elegance
His message of hope is sound
He cares for the least of us
And dreams of a world at peace
His stance is one of strength
Holds fast that he'll see wars cease
Walks with the common folk
Dines with those graced with wealth
Treats each with great dignity
Promises each their share of health
The world is in such disarray
Yet as he loves his own
He pledges to help end our strife
And bring calm to our homes
Bless us, Bless him

Jacqualynn Prettyman
*Phoenix, AZ*

## A Journey

A summer shower
While tickling our senses
Surprises our eyes with rainbows

Yet heavy liquid drops in autumn
Dislodge an endless tapestry of leaves
Filling our hearts with longing

Winter hail
Covers paths of uncertainty
Freezing human steps beyond movement

Until spring arrives
Cradled in embryonic possibilities
Revealing puddles of hope

Like water entering a safe harbor
We continue our journey
And embrace faith

Like water, we are all on a journey

Madge Reilly
*Staten Island, NY*

## Flight of the Hummingbird

Tiny aviators with colors seen as if through a kaleidoscope
Sunbeams illuminate their prisms
Flickering of tongues salivate, thirsting for ambrosia
Scents of sweet nectar enticing urgency
Beckoning as a lighthouse
the navigators search and seek
Dancing to and fro as if ballerinas,
gently, elegent, yet frenzied tempo
Graceful, Hummers sing on a quiet breeze
the tune they alone own.
All efforts have not been in vain
Miles all around it is now within reach
All needs for this hunger will fulfill
Energy to the necessity to their survival
Their ultimate orgasmic urgency will be complete
For they have found the color of this ambrosia
Red Red Red

Dolores Hurley
*Hartshorne, OK*

I can remember my love of reading all the way back to kindergarten. My mother is an avid reader, as are all my five sisters. The classic "Golden Books," Raggedy Ann and Andy, The Gingerbread Man, Mother Goose Nursery Rhymes, and the Hobbitt, etc. Reading is knowledge, adventure, make believe, and will forever be a treasure in my daily life until my existence on Earth ceases.

# The River

The water runs freely so blue and so deep
It's a beautiful sound that will lull you to sleep.
You see the wild life in the water so free
What a wonderful sight for anyone to see.
There's no place on Earth with a more beautiful sight
As the birds grouped together enjoying their flight.
Then comes the rain and the snow so abound
The animals and birds are not to be found.
My water now swift and gray from the sand
You can see the rocks moving as fast as they can.
Now as you watch from my river banks
I send you a warning that's ever so frank.
Stay away from my water it's dark, deep and cold
Whoever comes in forever I hold.
When the water is rushing through the channel in anger
Stay away from my banks and place not a finger.
But when the spring comes and the trees turn to green
Now the birds and the wildlife are here to be seen.
Run, play in my waters so calm and abound
Before winter comes without making a sound.

Dessie Cadd
*Welches, OR*

## You Helped a Friend Who Really Needed You

What kind of words can I say
What award could I ever give
To such a special friend
Who can give a person a reason to live

You've shared all of my good times + my bad times too
And you've given me so much love
So I know our friendship is true

I wish I could repay you with money
Or a roomed filled with gold
But I can only say "Thanks"
For lifting my heavy load

Consider yourself sunshine
That brightens everyone's day
For it is your smile
That always leads the way

If you ever get discouraged
Or feel you can't make it through
Just remember inside, "you helped a friend who really needed you"

Mattie Garrett
*Sterling, IL*

# Untitled

I'm sitting mesmerized looking out a window at the dining of the birds
Having breakfast at the feeder; some a twosome, some in "herds."
I'm fascinated, no pun intended, a pecking order is in view
While a squirrel, not so patiently, waits he thinks for his due.

First the sparrows line the perch with bravado and greed;
Eventually pushing off those who are getting more seed.
You can definitely tell which sparrows persevere,
For some are so fat, they're barely clinging, that's clear.

Next the cardinal, so special, all husband and wife-like—
She's submissive but scaring out sparrows, he's ready to strike.
The bright red male of course fills his stomach first,
But guards the feeder for his mate after sating his thirst.

Time has gone by and the small meek birds sneak in.
There are juncos and chickadees and others, all of their kin.
They are also in pairs, extremely bashful and shy.
They barely sit, just grab a seed and then off they fly.

The birds, even the squirrel, are capricious with some human-like traits;
All captivating with their reserve, wariness, glutton, love and/or hate.
I've really enjoyed this analysis of nature and time,
And of course the urge and ability to put it in rhyme.

Marilynn Ingram
*Aurora, IL*

# Ugly

You tell me I am beautiful
You tell me I am smart
But when I look into the mirror I disgust myself

You tell me I am spectacular
I am so wonderful, if I am so wonderful
Why don't I look like her?

You see her in the magazines
You see her on TV
You see her on the hip hop videos that are on MTV

You tell me I am gorgeous, I am so radiant
You tell me I can be everything, that I am so intelligent
I really think your fibbing because a girl like me
Can't compare to her, the girl in the magazine

But if you say I am gorgeous
If you say I am smart
It will take some time for me to realize that
I don't have to be the girl on the cover of Vogue
I need to be me and to accept all my flaws
And love me for me.

Atasha B. Clay'Pena
*Oakland, CA*

# The Call

I felt the tenderness, the aching, the twinge of fear.
The night creeps up on me. The moonlight outlines my shadow
as the cool autumn breeze blows upon my shivering flesh,
my eyes take in the setting:

crisp leaves upon the broken trees,
the soft feel of the grass, lustrous in the full moon.

I try to let the guilt pass.
Nevertheless, it lies upon my skin like that of a weed
in the soft soil of my bluegrass home.
As I walk upon the dusky path of the dull woods,
I come across a defeated flower—its petals are scattered upon the path,
allowing submission to harsh conditions.

Somehow, I understand the passing of autumn shall fade
into winter that will have its cold, dark days—
with its murky, abandoned waters,
no children upon the rivers,
no deer grazing upon the fields,
no farmers out to tend to their earth.

The robin will soon come, greeting the misty morning,
singing its sweet melody to those, "it is spring,"
softly heard throughout the woods.
The early morning shower retorts with its gentle grace.
Oddly enough, the sweet robin justly confirms:
the start of something beautiful has begun.

Elaine Douglas
*Mooresville, IN*

I am twenty-one years old. I grew up in a suburban town in Kentucky. I am the youngest of three sisters. I have had a passion for writing since I can remember. Music helps inspire my poetry. The music and lyrics of a song can stir imagery and provide insight for a story, a poem or song lyrics. One simple word can often trigger the idea for a poem. My life experiences, emotions, and what I have learned fuse into my poetry. Life paves the passage way and is the key element to my writing.

# My Tree

The way God meant it to be
'Twas the summer of 1954
First cutting of alfalfa
Was the job in the store.
There right in the center
Of the field
A little cottonwood
Had started to grow!
No practical rancher
Would cut his yield
And let it grow.
But I did!
Now that tree towers
Above everything around
My tree
The way God meant it to be!

Helen Martens
*Atkinson, NE*

I am a retired teacher having taught for fifty-five years. I love the country where I have always lived just at the edge of the Nebraska Sandhills. The ranch work has always been a part of my life; helping harvest hay, checking and working with cattle, fixing fences, and the list goes on. Working with youth has enriched my life; helping with the 4-H, Scouting, and being a part of a saddle club for forty years as well as teaching has made me a happy, satisfied person.

# My Little Alley Cat

A little black and white bundle of fur and love was sent to me by
God, a special gift from Heaven alone
To help keep me happy, needed, warm and loved
She looks up at me with the most beautiful yellow, turquoise and green
eyes
I know she understands her purpose, she's very old and wise
She's been there for me thru thick and thin
I couldn't have a more true soul or a truer friend
She always looks to see what mood I'm in and quickly offers her playful
grin
She comforts me with purrs and love when I cry or when I'm blue
Without her love, well nothing else would ever do
I tell her I love her over, and over, and over
More than the stars in the sky or the grass and the clover
I never grow tired of her pretty face, I just thank God for His mercy and
Grace
No one will ever take her place in my heart, never a comprise
She's now asleep, and I can no longer see her beautiful eyes
Because once you've had such a true love and a treasure
How could anything else ever measure?
It is my prayer to the Lord of lights, that he will do what is right
And on that day when it's time to go to my heavenly home
I will not leave my dear friend on the earth alone
I pray to God she can come home with me,
There together we will spend eternity.

Tanya Liesse-Larsen
*Greeley, CO*

Tanya Liesse-Larson lives with her husband, their two cats, and two dogs. She is inspired
to write poetry by her mother and brother. She was inspired to write this poem by one
of her best friends who was a stray alley cat, hence the name of the poem. If the reader
could only know such a deep love and special relationship they too would be touched
forevermore.

# Uganda

An African country along the equator, a place where a foreigner will
need a translator. The city is fast paced, and living in the country
is a chore, but the suburbs you will crave more.

A land loaded with nighttime stars, a beautiful place where the
Dollar goes far. Open food markets, packed taxis, and police with
AK 47s. Yes, they have the gun power to send ya to heaven.

An African country with beautiful inhabitants with a black shine. I
mean they will show you hospitality with their last dime. An
African people among most who revere GOD, and this isn't a
façade.

The ex-home of the lade Idi Amin. A country that I have seen, a
place with Africans, Arabs, Europeans and possibly some Koreans.
A part of the mother-land flowing with milk, honey and oil, a
country that Idi Amin led into turmoil.

A distant country about 10,000 miles away and scandalized worse
than O.J. A beautiful country, I labored in the summer of '93 and
it was adventurous to me.

Michael D. Henderson
*Chicago, IL*

## Insanity

I think I'm going crazy
I'm driving myself insane
I'm bleeding so much blood
I'm dying with too much pain

There must be so much evil
I'm guessing too much hate
I can't believe my eyes
This is too much for one person to take
My smile's always hidden
Behind an evil glare
My eyes and face covered
by my long dark blackened hair.

Hell has opened doors for me
My name upon their script
people are just waiting for me
To make a mistake and trip.

Monsters hidden inside the dark
Skrieking with an evil laugh
Haunting my every dream with
It's madness and uncontrolled raft.
My soul is lost and can't be found
I wonder where it's gone
My spirit lingers here wide
Singing my melancholy death song.

Jocelyne Torres
*Hanover Park, IL*

# Poisoned by the Night

When the robin's songs cease
And the brilliance of light is vanquished
When the subtle wind
Becomes a piercing noise on my skin

I have been poisoned by the night.

When the squirrels no longer wrestle with leaves
Pouncing then teetering
From limb to limb
When all that remains
Is a scratching, clawing, breech to my serenity

I have been poisoned by the night.

When the air becomes sinister
Gnawing at my nose and ears
Chafing them to the raw
When the stillness becomes a torrent
Sweeping my mind into obscenities
Dark and violent

I have been poisoned by the night.

When patience escapes
Urged then willed through cracks
Squeezed by the pressure of darkness
When pleasantries and tidings of well-wishing
Are hustled past, through, and over

We have all been poisoned by the night.

Norman E. Harris, Jr.
*Groton, CT*

# This Time

"I wish I were younger, thinner, and just not the same."
The misconceptions we all have are so lame.
We should take pride in ourselves, don't be scared.
Everyone is beautifully different not to be compared.
Don't be ashamed show them what you're made of.
It's something everyone could use, it's called love.
Care about each other don't judge or put down.
Get people to smile more often not frown.
Why can we be so hurtful to those we care for?
Of course we're humans, but we're so much more!
We're brothers, sisters, moms and dads
so let us not waste time on stupid fads.
Don't follow the crowd and do things you shouldn't.
If you listened in the first place, you know you wouldn't
have fallen into temptation, but don't let it drag you in.
Who cares what you did before? This time you can win!
Keep your heart strong and your head held high.
Next time you won't be sitting there asking yourself why.

Chrystal Williams
*Sandusky, OH*

# My Main Man

Let me tell you a story about my main Man,
He can change your life no one else can.
His name is Jesus.  He's my Savior and King.
And of His praises, I would like to sing.
He came to Earth and was crucified,
For our sins, He suffered and died.
It doesn't matter how bad you've been,
If you'll repent of your sins, He will take you in.
Give Him a chance, and He'll change your life,
You'll find peace and joy—not trouble and strife.
He'll help you live in a Godly way,
If you'll talk to Him as you start each day.
He wants to help you and be your guide.
Give Him your life, and He'll walk by your side.
He'll never forsake you nor leave you alone,
You can count on Him for your soul He'll own.
He gave us the Golden Rule with which to live by,
He said you can love your neighbor if you'll just try.
The Bible tells us about His life and work.
If you live like Him, then you won't be a jerk.
If you'll trust in Him will all your heart and soul,
Your name will be inscribed on that everlasting roll.
And when at last you reach that promised shore,
You'll dwell with Him in Heaven forever and evermore.

Elizabeth A. Noe
*Lake City, AR*

## Lake Village

Being here today
among the cats, fields and fishermen
going to the water
if only to look at it,
Green and full of white birds.
The wind has blown limbs
down this morning
November to December gales
Forming hot
forming cold
moving dynamically across water
later the crickets find
a place to sing.
Even today
green lettuce and wasps are
Fresh and black signs
Finding growth
among bright red's leaves
and winter's white lights.

Stephanie Howell
*Lake Village, AR*

## Legacy of Love

It was a cold December morning when we got the news.
The matriarch that we loved so much, passed away while
we snoozed.
My mother's tears and passionate scream, cut through my
breast to my heart.
I cried for her as she phoned her sisters sobbing feverishly
in the dark.
Her voice sounded so melancholy, her body so restrained,
I could not imagine the depth of her emotional pain.

My brother and my sisters gathered in the den crying on each
other's shoulders. But to me my pain seemed to be overshadowed
by my desire to comfort my mother.
I had never seen such pain in her eyes, her heartfelt sorrow
expressed in her sighs.

Thelma Rhoda Ramsey Jones we loved you so much.
I would give anything to hear your voice, to feel your loving touch.
When I think of you I will not be sad for the legacy of your loving
heart will always make me glad.

From this world of pain and sorrow you have departed.
In my memory and heart you will remain young, vibrant, and beautiful
forever.

Aaron Bryant
*Theodore, AL*

This poem is dedicated to the memory of a remarkable woman named Thelma Roda
Lewis. She was my grandmother. She was a homemaker and wonderful wife. She loved
God and the church. She lived her life helping her family and neighbors. Her life was a
love for service to God. She was my friend and she was an excellent cook. She sewed
and knitted. I will remember her smile and laughter for the rest of my life. She was a
loving mother of eleven children. She lived to see five generations. May she rest in
God's loving arms.

# Majdanek

I gazed at the ashes that had lingered
over the many years.  A stale smell
was there.  Or was it my imagination?
My footsteps traced the round cylinder,
vast in size.

The steel dome rose above and protected me
from the rain.  The grey of the day was
matched only by the grey of pulverized dust
mingling in that pit, a somber witness
to the world.

Peering into the haunting tabernacle of death,
I saw the ashes that had become a symbol of darkness.
I felt the despair and the prayers and the tears
of each precious soul who made the mistake
of being a Jew.

I was alone and stepped into the rain to feel
water on my face.  It blended with my tears.
Nothing could ever wash away the pain of
these spirits.  They were mothers and fathers,
sisters and brothers.

My grandfather was among them.


Lorraine Twardowski
*Wilmington, DE*

## Bittersweet Journey

When colorful rainbows and blazing sunsets are no longer quite enough
And the gentle world I used to know is no more
When life's unrealized dreams have finally come and gone
And the soul is but a ripple on a wave on a distant shore
I will then try and find my solace in the yesteryears that might have been
And the tomorrows soon to pass in the warmth of a summer wind
And only then can I bid a fond farewell
To loves and tender moments I embraced so dear and true
And the smiles not lightly forgotten of friends and lovers I once knew
And when the echoes of children's laughter no longer can be heard
And those chubby faces with endearing hearts are but misty memories
Of the times gone by much too fast too soon
Like the ancient mariner who yearns to once again
Return home to the sea
I too will make my final exit
From a life both bitter and yet so sweet
With no regrets but that the journey once traveled was much too short a
retreat

Janice Ridge
*Hull, MA*

My history dates back to the '50s. Writing was not my major in college, but I was involved with the Fine Arts Committee and had the opportunity of inviting reknown poets to our college—I was quite impressed with Robert Bly, a lovely gentleman, and enjoyed his readings. I spent some of my younger years before marriage and divorce in Greenwich Village following the poets and writers when they had readings—not a Hippie, but a Bohemian spirit and soul at heart. As editor of my school newspaper I had the opportunity to share my articles and writings. I am an avid reader of non-fiction and poetry. I did write human interest and local articles for a while and even got paid and had a by-line. My favorite poets are Edna St. Vincent Millay and Rod McKuen. My favorite writers are F. Scott Fitzgerald and Hemingway.

# The Fog

The fog creeps into the city
On stealthy feet.
It sits hunched, waiting,
Then moves quietly on,
Putting forth damp tendrils
Which turn sharp outlines
Into ill-defined visions.
With its dull knife
It cuts large chunks
Out of city noises,
And the glare of neon lights
Becomes a soft blur.
Its moist fingers touch the face
Of the weary commuter
And stifle his silent cry
With warm oppressiveness;
Then it rolls on
Out into the harbor
And disappears,
Leaving a starlit sky
In its tranquil wake.

Marion L. Foster
*Schenectady, NY*

# The Midlife Blues

For one brief moment, I enjoyed my youth
With red hair and freckles and a temper to boot.
In the next brief moment I knew I was old
With gray highlights, and wrinkles, and the same temper, I'm told.
Of course I deny it; I'm the nicest person I know,
I can smile when I want to; I've learned to go with the flow.
I regret I can't ride with the top down anymore,
My double chin flaps in the wind 'til it's sore.
My wild oats have turned into All-Bran and prunes,
It's a moving experience and it keeps me in tune.
I just hate it when they say, "Want a senior discount?"
I guess I'll get used to it, there's no need to pout.
At least I can save a little cash along the way,
I can add it to my pension, and take a cruise someday.
Yeah right, I can barely afford my hormones these days,
But I can't afford not to, I'm mean as a snake.
Sorry if it seems like I'm in a bad mood,
But from now on I'm doing what I want to do.
It's just that life is too short and before I'm out of time,
I want to find peace instead of losing my mind.
So I've signed up for Medicare, decked out in purple and red,
To make a statement to the world, that I'm a long way from dead!

Suzanne Spencer
*Louisville, KY*

170

# Colors

To many of the human race,
Only Black and White occupy worldly space.
Hard and cold are these blank lives,
A single-minded choice, no will to compromise.

But beyond the realms of this blatant void
Is a world of animation, color, and joy.
Imagination bursts with wondrous dreams
Endless possibilities reveal anticipated beginnings.

Expanding the horizon, colors emphasize life,
The one reason to keep going through pain and strife
Colors make rainy days seem safe and warm,
Finding that sparkle in the midst of a storm.

The mind functions in a fascinating way,
The choices made affect life's rhythm every day.
Color, though, is perhaps the greatest choice of all,
Because color is the difference between life big and life small

Abby Specht
*Littleton, CO*

# Gift of Life
## A tribute to Ernest Hemingway who cheated all mankind

A man has rights
That are foreordained
These rights has he
From God obtained...

Freedom to choose
A way of life
Peace and justice
A choice of strife...

Values and goals
Are among a few
He has decisions
With what to do...

To make a home
And pick a wife
To take a stand
But not his life...

Dan Ninemire
*Denver, CO*

# A Gift in My Life

You are a gift in my life
in so many ways.
You are a place
I can always go for comfort.
You make me feel as though someone
is honestly interested in my life,
my worries, my fears—
the things that matter to me.
You remind me of something
I forget at times these days.
That someone actually cares about me.
and that I am loved.
You are what I have been waiting for,
But never had…
that answer to my prayers.
You are someone who cares enough,
to unlock for me,
the treasure of love,
and show me the secrets of my heart.
And you taught me something
that I never knew,
never suspected could exist.
How it feels
to be loved.

David L. Matthews
*Scottsdale, AZ*

## A Hand

I am writing a poem with my right hand.
I am writing a poem about a hand
The hand has five fingers holding a pen
The pen is a long stick with five fingers at the end.
The fingers are writing
Writing a poem
A poem with no ending about a hand

Lindsey M. Boyd
*Gilroy, CA*


## Anger

Anger is a funny thing
It comes up like a storm
And camps out in your home
Takes you through many changes
like the counselors
And many people say
It's not worth the rainy jailhouse stay
or the courthouse day
Not to mention the money you have to pay
In my mind
It could be managed in a different way
So I'm taking these classes
To watch, learn and pray.

Angel McMillan
*Birmingham, AL*

174

## Listen and Stop

Statistics and doctors want us to know
That smoking is a strict no-no
Everyone hears this message too
And knows what they really should not do.
Despite this warning, many still smoke,
And know for good health it's not okydoke.
This little verse is not a joke,
It's a serious warning not to smoke.

Ferol Redman
*Homewood, IL*

## You Complete Me

The day has come when you arrived
seeing your face brought tears to my eyes
At first I was scared
But then I saw your little eyes
Looking back at me
You gave my finger a squeeze
And suddenly you put my mind at ease.
The world seemed like it stopped
My world was bright
I slowly kissed your head goodnight
While I was lying there ready to sleep
I thought to myself how much you
Complete me

Stephanie Rinaldi
*Marathon, FL*

# What I Like

I like the birds and trees
The flowers and the breeze
The blue of the sky
And the clouds that pass by.

The smell of the pine
The forest so fine
I love the autumn leaves
And the rush of mighty seas.

Audrey A. Renna
*Milton, FL*

# My Little Boy Blue

A little boy just four years old
My love for him just grows and grows.
This little boy with eyes so blue,
Steals my heart you know it's true.
His smile is like the sunshine bright
On days as dark as midnight
He romps and plays the whole day long.
Until all light of day is gone.
Then when the night turns into dawn,
He awakes with a sleepy yawn
Ready to renew his play
Until the day has passed away.

Pam Davis
*Iuka, MS*

# It's Not in the End

As I finally reached the end hoping I could find rest,
I looked and found nothing,
Nothing but my deep emptiness,
I thought I would get past it,
Thought maybe it would disappear,
That along with my greatest enemy
And my worst fear,
Hoping maybe I was lost
I looked back and saw everything I had missed,
So much beauty and happiness,
So many smiles and laughter I had missed,
Every day I forgot to live,
I thought it's what I had aimed for,
It's what I was trying to achieve,
In the end though,
I realized that I had been deceived,
By who else but my worst enemy,
The one I was running from all along,
The one I can never escape,
The only one I hate,
Me

Yolanda Devenpeck
*Ontario, CA*

## September 11, 2007

I awoke and felt different today, I did not know why?
The day was bright and the birds sang as they flew up in the sky.
I took my shower, got dressed and headed out the door.
But then I saw a newspaper and it dropped me to the floor.

September 11th happened six years ago today!

The events of that day still haunt us, our country is still crying.
The pictures will never ever leave our minds, our children will grow up sighing!
That we a country so great and strong, must live in terror now!
But we re-build and fight for freedom forever and wherever how.

Our men and women serve around the world in dangers way.
Their gift to us is freedom, we treasure it each day.
The price they pay is death, a footnote the papers say.
How can our country forget so quickly, the price that they must pay!

We are fighting in Iraq, our freedom challenged there,
Our young men and women fighting for us here
We question many times, what is over there?
Does it really matter, if they can threaten us over here!

Let us honor them with grace and dignity, and never forget their names.
They paid the ultimate price for freedom, it never is a game.
They do not get to come home at the end of a long, long day.
But, we go about our business and forget the price they have to pay!

September 11th happened six years ago today!

Tab F. Steinhaus
*Gurnee, IL*

I was inspired by Mattie J.T. Stepanek, poet and peacemaker. I found peace, strength, and relaxation in reading Mattie's poems. I started writing poetry to my wife and have not stopped. Like Mattie, I find the love of life all around me. I write poetry about a special event, a special day, a Cubs baseball game, a river through Pittsburgh. I also keep a journal of my life to remember and never to forget.

# Untitled

Like the awe of great strength in rare beauty reposing,
Inarticulate traveler first viewing the sea
And unable to verbally cherish the breakers,
Intends reverent silence devotion to be.

The sea with its fervor of tumult and strife
Insignificant man with awe overpowers.
Its mighty waves lashing out endlessly, fearlessly
Succumb to their greatness what tenor is ours.

In silence we worship the masterful sea;
Our words all are impotent, useless and void
Our tongues rendered soundless acknowledge their lack
In deepest humility, pure, unalloyed.

The sea now is peaceful; its stirring has ceased,
And calmly it laps at the rim of the sand.
It murmurs complacently, lulled into slumbering,
Gently aware of the charm of the land.

Yet still I am mute as its grace stops my throat
I am choked into silence by gratitude's sway
That the sea should so tenderly stoop to enfold me,
Holding me close to its bosom always.

And like to the sea, dear, is your love to me
Magnificent, wonderful, tender and kind;
A thing to be worshipped with discourse inadequate,
Silent because of the words I can't find.

Jane K. Grammer
*Shrewsbury, NJ*

Many years ago a young man and I were very much in love. I wrote this poem because I had never said "I love you" to any beau. But he was about to leave for the war in the pacific. He took this poem with him. He didn't make it back, but it helped that he knew how much I cared.

# The Fear of the Unknown

What is this feeling that wanders
Through my mind, and lingers
In my subconscious most of the time?

It is hard to explain;
The answer is unfound
It feeds on my being and holds me down.

I've asked my mother
To see what she thinks,
She searched her heart
But couldn't find the link

Then I decided to ask my grandmother
Who is wise in her years,
And the answer she gave me
Brought me to tears
She told me,
"Sweetheart, don't get angry
About what you feel,
It's normal, and you are not alone,
Everyone has the fear of the unknown."

Dominique Smart
*Brooklyn, NY*

# I Love You

I have been looking for you all my life.
Intimately searching for a chance at happiness.
Long ago our souls forged an ancient path, we've forever walked.
Loving you is sunrise and sunset, full of adventure and ritual.
One that creates a bond, heartfelt speaking without words.
Only you can feel me, even find me while I sleep.
Visions of elegant beauty encircle, as we float among clouds.
Visiting and empowering within the landscapes of slumber
Every day, despite distance, our hearts whisper to one another.
Each night, a union perfected in the realm of dreams
You have given me hope and opened my heart to endless possibilities.
Your love has brought harmony and joy to my world.
Out in the darkness, I lived, forgotten by life and love.
Obscuring the dark, with kindness and laughter, you walked to my side.
United are we, by oath and spirit, a journey of hearts and faith.
Under God, we walk hand-in-hand, watching life's magic unfold.

Faith Seely
*Las Vegas, NV*

# Untitled

What makes the mourner turn away,
from the grave, with a tear in his eye;
Or two friends that are parting at the
end of the day, not wanting to say goodbye,
what makes a man read a sonnet, by a poet
whose time was remote, and cause him
to stop for a moment, with just a lump in his throat.
What makes the painter, as he watches
the sun ride golden in the skies,
paint with his brush, a picture, that's
alive even after he dies.
Some call it love, some, inspiration,
and some say it's just how you feel.
But without a doubt, there's a
spark in us all, and whatever it
is—it's real.

Rod Annas
*Schaumburg, IL*

# Could It Be?

If a bell rang out a reminder of peace
Would the sound vibrate feelings unleashed
Happy responses living in a world content
A place where our problems could find a vent
Color undistinguished like a photo that fades
Our differences flexible as tall grass blades
Hatreds could shrink like grapes left on the vine
Humbleness reigns, causing big egos to decline
War would lose it's meaning, a thing of the past
Where hands could join hearts completely at last
Our globe a home connected, no barriers or walls
Where we've mastered its keeping a shelter for all
How many times would the bell have to chime
To remind us don't wait even with mountains to climb
If love and caring became as natural as it should be
Then peace on this Earth could become a reality!

Dorothy Dunn
*Denver, CO*

# On the Edge of Faith

Moments there are when the light shines through
And assurance and hope are born anew,
When a breath of prayer opens wide the door
To infinite Grace and its treasure store.

When to forgive completely seems within my grasp
And the forgiving hand of God I dare to clasp,
When I feel I could find a sure direction
To bring from ashes a resurrection.

Such moments compassion swells in the heart of me,
And I reach out to the world with every part of me.
The thought of injustice brings a stab of pain,
And I would march in the ranks for Right again.

Moments are I can measure the pulse of the throbbing earth
And believe that forever there will be rebirth.
Then the sea and the land seem one with me,
And I'd be at home when this world is done with me.

Such moments I would open my heart, my hands, and my brain;
I'd shed resentment and fear and love of selfish gain;
I'd be better and stronger and truer every day;
I would walk with the King on the King's Highway!

Moments there are…

Mildred Miles
*Kingston Springs, TN*

# Who I am, Who are you

The "secret" is out
On who I am, but
Most people think,
That it's just another scam.

I can be, anyone and anything,
I choose to be
Just by using my thoughts,
They are free.

I choose with my thinking,
To have everything I desire
All I have to do is ask, believe, and acquire.

I know this "SECRET" is true,
Because, I have most everything,
I ever ask for, and it's all like new,
And that's my clue.

The "SECRET" is true!

Now, you can use the "SECRET" too!
To become a new, successful, wealthy, and
Thoughtful you!

And this makes me ask, "WHO ARE YOU"?

Vikki Xanders
*Lore City, OH*

# If Only

You in your chair, I'm in mine.
Your life in yours
mine in mine.
What you see from yours
is different
from what I see from mine.
Not because of the positions
of the chairs.
But because of the positions
of our lives.
If only we could change chairs
If only you could sit in mine.
and I in yours.
Maybe take over each other's lives
and live as the other for a while.
If only we could change our lives
So easily as changing chairs.
If only.

Jane Pallat
*Seward, NE*

# Right Lane North to Piru

Monday morning this highway-phantom grabbed the wheel
Turning it, see it sure wasn't me, unless something sly
Rousted my gray-matter… like an electronic sparking
Of the sludge attending mundane matters of getting to
The company… nothing pertinent, see.

Nothing like what we'd see after "He" turned onto the
Ramp north-bound to Piru, and went over the rusting
Bridge built in the '30s, actually.

Below was only beige sediment poked with switches of river-
Birch, obedient between mothering arms of sculpted banks
Polka-dotted with pudding stones.

Perhaps this phantom ordains me to see something pertinent
Today… something impervious to the speeding bullet progress
Of science. Maybe that linen-gray horse off the road on the left,
Cotton eyed, bucolic, back swayed like a summer hammock…
Brittle hoofs in dead stubble… His grave soon to be, probably.

Maybe that stand of corn up on the right, stripped of kernel and
Shuck, flapping like old buffalo parchment… plumb useless now, see.
Or that old cat slumped in the pine of somebody's porch over there…
Grizzled fur, bone lean haunches… hurting bone I mean!
"He" drove me home about four… nothing's changed, missing my shift?
Sheez, not indispensable, ME?!

Virginia Garner
*Post Falls, ID*

187

# If My Arms Were Long Enough

If my arms were long enough
I'd fold you to my breast, dear Earth,
And tuck fresh atmosphere around your face
I'd kiss the spots where forests were clear cut
Where rich farmland is rutted with erosion
I'd wipe pollution from your skies
And brush away the pests that cause you pain
Then weep a gentle, healing rain
If my arms were long enough

Alice A. Reese
*Columbia, MO*

# Treatment of the Trees

Can you hear the rustle in the wind as the trees blow?
Can you feel the light radiating from the sun's glow?
The trees sing a little song.
You can hear it when summer days are long.
The trees whisper their secrets to you.
Of a forgotten time when the earth was new.
When outside I think of the sad story they tell.
A story about nature before the forests fell.
The trees are cut down for more materials and wood.
This life we are living cannot be good.
How often do you listen to the tree's song?
Not listening to their tale just seems wrong.

Franciszka Stopa
*Alamogordo, NM*

# Virgo

Most people are in a hurry & dazed.
Our grand babies live for computers.
Our six-year-olds driving scooters.
Our lives moving ahead so fast,
Our memories let us hold onto the past.
Being me is cool and all good,
Please let me be understood.
But in charge for even a day,
Only as a sweet butterfly way.
May I live long enough to see,
You never know!
A world hunger and war free.

Jackie McIntosh
*Newark, OH*

I really love that life can be written down when you think of it, never to be forgotten.
This way your family and friends can always have a wider range of who you really were
other than just a picture. My family and I are really close. They often ask me how much
do I have going on in my head. I certainly wish I had all the answers. My penmanship is
horrible and I am not as educated as I'd like to be in vocabulary. Poetry seems to bring
out the inner need to be me.

## Labyrinth

Miles across the water I walked
Stalking the waves, unfettered by the
Riptides, undaunted by the depths of the Sea.
This obscene obsession obliterates my vision
It is my hoax alone or a hoax for future generations?
For one nanosecond the heathens rejoice in the
Presence of the hangman.

The gauntlet has been presented
Rounds of battles must be fought,
Struggles won, lives lost.
What assurance is there of no betrayal,
Is it best they leave their posts by
Attrition or by slaughter?

Censorship you say,
Alas, will it protect the evil doers,
The nay Sayers or the true innocents?

Miles across the water I walked
Stalking the waves, unfettered by the
Riptides, and undaunted by the depths of the Sea.
And yes, Miracles do happen.

Laila Amatullah
*New York, NY*

## To Do the Impossible

It's possible to do the impossible!
Because it's possible no giving up
Trying to do the impossible!
So if you think of giving up before
You try doing something impossible!
Always think it's possible to do this impossible!
Also the impossible might be possible
If in back of your mind!
If you know it really is possible to do the impossible

Lawrence Constantine
*Medford, MA*

## A Sterling Creation

I weave my own strand in
The web of existence,
being responsible for
my response to this
time of transition and
challenge.
When I withhold from life
a void is created,
but when I give to it
no one can change
nor remove
the everlasting result.

Becky Olvera
*Woodland, CA*

## Cousin Reunion

Cousins share so many things
As life goes by we realize
The heritage we share together
We have from birth until we die
It's wonderful to reunite and
Precious are these days so few
The bonds of Family ~ still there
The love and friends ~ we just renew
There was a time we were the young
But now with all our parents gone
The time has come ~ we take their place
Rightfully, where we belong
Our hearts are full with gratefulness
For God has blessed us all the way
By giving us a special time and
Giving us this Special Day ~

June Felt
*Babson Park, FL*

## Our Song

Be kind and gentle
Express love openly and fully,
Voice your beliefs with directness, honesty, and humility
And be mindful that Truth cannot be contained in only your voice

Stay strong and be yourself
Especially in times demanding change
Keep rhythm with the song within.
For this song is yours, a gift.
Listen; Love; Dance; Sing; Enjoy

Beth Pope
*Phoenix, AZ*

## Same Old Song

I thought you didn't need me,
I knew you didn't care
why would you if you had put me through all that pain and despair?
My life was the book
you were the page
I thought I could just tear you out when I didn't want you there
at one point I needed you
but how could you come back after I kept you gone for so long?
That's when I realized you were right and I was wrong you were right
there where I left you all along
still singing your sweet old song

Amanda Pagano
*Briarwood Queens, NY*

# White Winter's Day

Come sit around the fireplace
and have a little chat
For the snow is falling heavily
So hang up your tweed hat

A cup of tea is on the stove
to warm you up inside
We can reminisce of old days
While we sing a tune and smile

It's been years since I've seen you
the days have past away
Can we catch up on everything
Or will we just merely be able to say

That I think of you often
and the thought makes me smile
For even though we've gotten old
We can still send love across the miles

So with the crackling of the embers
and as the conversation halts
With the cup of tea that did warm me
Comes to an end once more

We part our ways as we usually did
and give each other one last grin
and say we'll see each other again
On a white winter's day.

Maureen Corry
*Somers, NY*

## It Used to Be

Sometimes
in spring
when gentle winds
would carry to your windows
sweet scent of flowers
and newborn leaves
the mind is able
to relive forgotten treasures
of the past—
the games you played
the loves you loved
the roads you walked.
Sometimes
in spring
when you stand still
in front of open windows
away from struggle
craving and routine
the mind is able
to relive what now you call
It used to be

Cornel Paunescu
*Cincinnati, OH*

# All in the Act

It's all in the act,
they say.
An act to impress
without putting yourself
too out there.

Hiding.
Deceiving.
"Little" white lies.

I wonder
what
who
is really behind that mask
you wear?
Is it just
too good to be true?
Are you just that good
Of an actor?

Christine Le
*Florence, KY*

# Stars

Up in the clear dark night
The stars glow so bright
They can lead you to so many places
While they cover so many spaces
I imagine they have bright smiling faces
With shoes that have laces

Morgan Thielman
*Hainesport, NJ*

# The Defense

On the shore dimly seen through the mists of the deep,
Where the foe's haughty host in dead silence reposes,
What is that which the breeze over the towering steep,
As it fitfully blows, now conceals, now discloses?
Now it catches the gleam of the morning's first beam,
In full glory reflected, now shines on the stream.

And where is that band who so valiantly swore,
That the havoc of war and the battles confusion,
A home and a country should leave us no more?
Their blood has wiped out their foul footsteps pollution,
No refuge could save the hireling and slave,
From the terror of flight, or the gloom of the grave.

Jincy Thomas
*Deer Park, NY*

## What Is a Poet?

A poet is a possessor of mystery, originality,
and humor—who loves the world and all it
holds, reaps pleasure and enjoyment being young
or being old.

A poet is a recorder of beliefs about life,
whose expressions can be of emotion or grief—
using rhythm or rhyme to express his images as
they spring into memory—presenting an imaginative
array of belief.

A poet possesses patience and much insight,
capturing the charm and beauty of nature with
reflections while in flight—is perceptive to all
thoughts as they come to mind, seeks an outlet in
language of verse, called poetry, which can last for
many lifetimes.

Martha Wood
*Angleton, TX*

Education: High School and Business School graduate  Occupation: Retired Office Manager  Interests: Family, Grandchildren, Writing, Reading, Volunteering, Traveling, and Sports  My inspirations are from everyday experiences. My favorite poets are: Carl Sandburg, Robert Burns, and John Keats  Publication: *Oriental Flower in Poetic Voices of America*, 1998. I was inspired to write the poem submitted after attending a Poetry Festival whereby the question "What is a poet?" was asked and never answered.

# A Journey with the Lord

In the quiet dawn when all was still,
God spoke to me and calmed my fears.
He gave me assurance to face the day,
Said He would go with me all the way.
He said just to trust Him and all would be well,
As long as I walked with Him, I could not fail.
He said go forward and never look back, for He made all
Creatures, whether large or small.
He cares for each one, He is Lord over all!

He rules the universe for both you and me,
He's King of the jungle, Master of the sea.
His greatness is felt through out the land, for He holds the world in
the palm of His hand.
He carries our burdens, He knows our sorrows, we need not worry about
tomorrow, for we have no promise beyond today, so live for Jesus today
and always.

He'll guide your footsteps, your mind and soul,
He'll give you peace and joy that the world does not know.
So take hold of His hand and keep trudging on,
For it won't take long till you reach heaven's shore.
Then you can sit down with a sigh of relief and say it's all been
worthwhile
Just to sit at Jesus' feet.

Vera R. Morrison
*Cheryville, NC*

# A Natural Love

When the sun sets in the evening sky,
Your love lights up like a starry night.
I feel the warmth from the starlit glow,
Much like the love that you bestow.
I see the colors that nature brings.
Your love to me is just like spring.
My love for you is like a new beginning.
I need your love, a love never-ending.
When I look in your eyes of brown,
It's just like seeing a starry crown.
Darling, my life has been so void,
Of true love and much joy.
But now I see what love is about.
Your love to me, I can't do without.
Someday soon, we can start our journ,
And share the love that we so yearn.
So take my hand as we dance along.
Along life's way, singing a song.
Singing a song, in harmony
Dancing along, you and me.
As I end this poem I write to you,
Remember one thing I say to you,
I love you.

Jay Green
*Chatsworth, GA*

200

# Life's Path

I often ponder life as a whole,
And wonder whether it was due to my soul.
The lives before was I good or bad,
and how strong an effect they really had.
There have been many difficulties to overcome
some days seem so bleak,
My spirituality maintains my strength,
when I begin to go weak.
I hold on to my faith and truly believe all
problems will run their course.
I never forget that we are guided by a
benevolent powerful force.
In our lifetime there are many lessons we need to learn
Once all is completed, we can guide others from Heaven
and never need to return.

Sheila M. Cooperman
*Boca Raton, FL*

## Mother Love

One thousand miles of anxiety
Trying to get to you
Before your weary heart gives out.
Now I sit mournfully
Holding the hand that rocked my cradle
And wiped my tears.
Your hand, arthritis-gnarled, age-spotted,
That worked its fingers raw
Mothering your clamoring brood of seven.
Though widowed in your prime
You sought no pity for your lot.
Did you cry alone at night?
Did you fold your hands in supplication
And ask for strength and tender mercy?
Tell me more about Dad, I'd say.
But reticence was your way.
Do you feel my presence?
I love you, Mom, I sigh,
Stroking your still-pink cheeks,
Watching you breathe in strange rhythms
Until you are gone.
Yet I hold your hand as it turns ashen, then cold,
Aching for the stories left untold.

Sandy Hinz
*Great Falls, MT*

# My Medium-Sized Black Box

I have a medium-sized black box,
The kind used to store 5 by 7 index cards.
In it, I store pieces of useful information about life I have picked up
along the way.
I am a connoisseur of advice, you see
Ask me about relationships
And I will look under the 'R' section for a tidbit
Want a creative idea?
Under the 'I' section for "ideas" I have plenty to give.
How about the 'J' section?
You bet I have two tons of jokes to tell.

If I were on a desert island I would take my box, some index cards, and
some pens.
During calm moments I'd read the index cards in the box.
During energizing moments I'd add an index card to the box.
During sad moments I'd be uplifted by the ideas in the box.
During creative moments I'd invent a poem connecting two random
ideas in the box.
During reflective moments I'd appreciate all the different thoughts I have
in the box.
During bored moments, I'd create a card game using the cards found in
the box.

In case I lose the box, I wrote the following note on the bottom of the lid:
"Dear fellow student, please use this box to make yourself wiser,
Do share your own input, don't be a miser!
But after you have learned,
The box must be returned
To me—your favorite advisor"
(see index card titled "Address of Owner" in the 'A' section)

Lauren Silver
*East Brunswick, NJ*

# Examining Thoughts

"As thoughts would be produced,
one could assume that one
was producing thoughts,
as though one did not
already know.
So,
thoughts are produced up here
on the metropolis of Zanbuka
where all of us pondering thoughts
rest our fair bottom bodies
upon the sweetly soft and
enticing floor of the
Wonderful,
gigantic treetop leaves."

Andy Metzger
*Carlisle, PA*

# An Angel Named Terry

I had a wonderful friend named Terry
Who loved everyone, children especially
And they all adored her in return.
She was a special Angel to me.

She visited me without fail every Tuesday,
If it was raining, I'd say, "Let's skip today,"
But she'd reply, "I'll put on my raincoat
And come to visit you anyway."

One day she came in and asked, "Guess what
I had for lunch today? It was so good,"
"Peanut butter and banana sandwich,"
I said, "That was Elvis Presley's favorite food."

She couldn't wait to see Pope Benedict
when he came to New York in May,
It was very cold and windy out.
Terry wore two coats to Yankee Stadium that day.

If Terry made a promise she never broke it.
There could be a blizzard or tornado,
She never veered from a promise.
And kept a friend waiting in limbo.

That was my Angel Terry,
Kind, never rude or bold,
When God made Terry
He threw away the mold.

Helen M. Kerecz
*Dobbs Ferry, NY*

# Please Be Mine

Please be my refuge and keep me from harm.
I just want to rest secure in your arms.
Please be my shelter in times of storm.
Within your embrace I'll stay safe and warm.

Please be my sunshine when life turns to rain.
With my hand in yours I can handle the pain.
Please be my strength whenever I'm weak.
Without you beside me my future looks bleak.

It may seem like a lot to ask.
I'm sure it will prove to be no easy task,
But when it seems like too much to do,
Just remember that I'll do the same for you.

Bridget Laktash
*Wyoming, NY*

## Winter Weather

Snow for those who love its beauty,
Cold for those with outside duty,
Threat of severe weather—excitement for a few!
Rushes of adrenaline energize you.
Why do we love it—this time of year?
Because it's so different, brisk and severe.
We feel the wonder and tell our friends,
But always it too soon ends.
Now only fond memories remain,
Left only for memory lane.

Bill Lomas
*Duluth, GA*

## True Love

With her I found true love, my soul mate.
When we looked at each other, we melted in the essence of our
beings.
To touch was to feel an amazing energy that took us to another
world.
The magic of our kiss was transformed into fire and passion.
Making love was the culmination of our bodies, minds, hearts and souls.
Nothing can be greater than this love, for it reached the highest
mountain, traveled the far distances of the universe and back to
reality again.
With her I found true love, my soul mate.

Edwin Rios
*Brooklyn, NY*

## A Flash Prayer

Did you ever say a 'flash prayer' for a friend or foe?
Did you ever ask yourself could that person know?
If I said a short prayer to God to send His Love,
To the person impatiently waiting in line—trying not to shove,
Or the person driving a car at a terrific speed
Would they feel the blessing of Love, and take heed?
What a joyful feeling when we can give to someone
An unknown Blessing from the Father and Son
It just takes a minute or a few seconds, of our time
To give a 'flash prayer' to an unknown or sublime,
Next time you see someone struggling or just waiting in line
Give a 'flash prayer' for that person, and in time
The prayer you said for another, could be a blessing returned for you or
me
'Flash Prayers' are free to everyone you see.
Here's your chance to spread some love and glee.
Maybe it would be a good practice to pursue,
Give it a try, you've nothing to lose, it's all up to you.

Doris P. Auman
*Richland, PA*

## Wake Up Young Sisters

Wake up young sisters what's going on in your world today?
And why you stand by and allow the brothers to disrespect you this way?
The way I see it the brothers are in control, they're running the show.
Yet you say you are free, you're down with it, and you're in the know.
How long will it take before you open your eyes, take off the blinders
and realize?
The brothers have their own agenda it's all about them so don't be
surprised.

Everybody is looking for a quick fix; they want to be rich and they don't
care how.
They're willing to do anything for the money, and they want it now.
The rappers call you all kinds of names still you buy their tapes.
Your voice has no meaning: they spike your drinks and call it date rape.
You've lost your self-esteem, because they show you no respect.
You appear nude in their videos and continue to practice unsafe sex.

I ask you my sister; how much are you willing to give in the name of
love?
And if they were the ones having babies would they wear a glove?
The population would surely decrease if the roles were reversed.
Fact is: men will be men they tend to put themselves first.
Wake up young sisters what price are you willing to pay?
Any why do you allow the brothers to treat you this way?

We are all God's children and with a specific purpose in life.
We need each other to survive among the turmoils and strife.
You talk about your mothers and grandmothers and how much they gave.
How they worked, from sun up to sundown, and the sacrifices they made.
You'd never put up with that behavior, not in a million years, you say,
And yet you sisters are being exploited each and every day.

Cathleen McKinley
*Bloomfield, CT*

## August 19, 2008

The jagged edge
of deep surprise
stepped into view
without disguise
each silhouette
stood side by side
each line a guide
defining lies
the breath of
toxin air released
allowed each sleep
to feel at peace
awaken souls
reveal and see
your thoughts
determine
who to be

Helene D'Amato
*S. Windsor, CT*

# Dreams and Time

I've had a few dreams in my time, teaching
marrying, a kid or two.
I married young and soon God gave me
a wonderful son.
And all my dreams were coming true.
I needed more time, time for husband and home and my new little one.

But then along came more, a second son
and soon son number three.
Three sons to love and cherish and feed
And oh yes, "Mommy a hug and story just for me."
And so "Dear Lord, I prayed, give me more time, that's what I need."

As time went by, they grew and off to school they went
And as for me, time to dust off that teaching degree.
But to my surprise, son number four, another blessing God
had sent.
So back to 2 a.m. feedings, diapers & lullabies—will I ever have time for
me?

But before I knew it, one by one they were off in a flash it seems.
To college, to jobs, and children of their own.
Oh, I hope they have time—time for their dreams
As for me, now it's my time, time to pursue dreams I've not yet known.

But what do I do, I use my time waiting it seems,
For phone calls, a card or two, checking my email in hopes of hearing
from you.
My dreams, YOU ARE MY DREAMS!
Now I will have time, lots and lots of time
and only memories of my dreams—if only I knew.

Fran Good
*Aliq, PA*

## It Does Not Compute

My mind is so scrambled,
And I don't know if it's me or what,
I dialed this number 1-866-282-6587,
And 1-800-922-4684 was what I got.

I talked to one girl and tried to explain,
The reason I called; my order never came.
She transferred me to another,
Although polite and informed;
I began to wonder if I was scammed,
I should have been for-warned.
Too many oddities, over an order a month before,
A light stroke had hit me, that's no lore.
Have I been so out of it?
I don't want to appear a bore,
But tell me how this could happen?
Was the grim reaper a knocking at my door?

There's no similarity, my brain works overtime.
I just sit and wonder and try to make it rhyme.

Rose M. Prill
*Lorain, OH*

I'm eighty years old and have four daughters and a step-son. I also have four granddaughters, one grandson, and two great-granddaughters so far. I love to garden both vegetables and flowers, make crafts, enjoy sewing, and I even decorated all the wedding cakes for my children. I worked as a bookkeeper and stenographer. I am now a widow after fifty-two years of marriage. Now I have more time to crochet gifts for my family and write poetry. I have over eighty albums of photographs I've taken of family and vacations all over America. I play the piano and organ; I love older music. I've survived over forty surgeries from head to toe fighting cancer. When I can't sleep I write poetry.

# There's No Such Thing as Perfect

She was a girl, sweet and quiet
to a new school is where she came
sometimes feeling hurt, sometimes feeling shame
In many eyes she was just some perfect girl
little did the eyes know that she was different

There were people who wanted to be her,
but she would kill to be anything else,
Much more lived behind a pretty face
who tried so hard to stand tall,
tried so hard not to fall
If only people knew what went on in her world

Lost, was a father of hers
Lost, were friends that she'd loved
Lost, were the people who understood her best

All that was gained was pain
All that was gained was pain

She felt the pain which she never deserved
maybe some day it will leave her
People opened their eyes
and looked at her perfect world
but she knew, only she knew
that there's no such thing as perfect

Katie Hoelzer
*Massapequa, NY*

This poem comes straight from my heart and is very meaningful to me. It was inspired by real events that went on in my life when I was younger. I hope to continue writing and publishing my work. I also hope to inspire others out there. Poetry to me is one of the greatest forms of art. As Oscar Wilde once said, "It is through art, and through art only, that we can realize our perfections; through art and art only that we can shield ourselves form the sordid perils of actual existence."

# The Painting

six feet by six feet
hardwood stretchers braced
for eight ounce canvas
gesso primed surface
dammar varnish and thinner
rounds flats and brights
scumble playfully
with umbers and ochres
serious later
with cadmium reds and yellows
then nunaced
with cobalt blues and greens
unexpected revelations
and passages of paint
find their source
a stroke here
a dab there
every day
happily
refusing to be resolved
and the paint never dries

Paul Saberin
*Chambersburg, PA*

## Golden Years

They define that special time in a person's life as…
When everyday events are absent of strife.
Families have parted and are on their own
Emptiness and order fills each home.
Meaningless chores replace job duties of the past,
A dog, cat, or two fill the days with time-consuming tasks.
Daily business is predictable but ritual in nature
Hours pass as slowly as bills in the legislature.
Trips to each doctor hope to bring news of healthy joints and hearts,
Relying on Medicare and paying co-pays—necessary parts…
of that daily routine where every minute is a carbon copy of the one before
Only changing when a seldom-seen child enters the door.
Then the pure joy of life's blessings permeate each room
Making the house—a home free of gloom
of the monotony of being in one's golden years
Accompanied with experience, memories and abatement of fears.
Golden years—you come too fast!
Riding along as each life lasts!

Elaine M. Foglia
*Amity, PA*

# The Broken Heart

Going to school so happy, today was all about you.
For it was the day you were going, to figure out something new.
You could smile every second, until you could smile no more.
This was the day that on your test your percent would be ninety-four.
Your mom and dad helped you study, till your brain was completely
full.
For a test you could work with nobody, and you had to stay in control
When you got to school so happy, and settled down in your chair
You felt an ache within your heart; something was missing; it
seemed bare.
As seconds, minutes, hours passed, the pain, it just got worse.
"What could this be?" You thought to yourself,
Was this some kind of curse?
Your teacher left the room, for a phone call she must talk.
She headed toward the office, doing a fast-pace walk.
She came back to the classroom, some tears rolled down her cheek.
Your name she calls quite softly, shivering while she speaks.
You get out of your wooden chair and then you push it in.
Frightened you were in trouble, and scared you may have sinned.
You tiptoed to the teacher's desk, wondering what was wrong.
"Hunny," she whispered, wiping her tears, I'm trying to be so strong.
You looked at her confused, at what she was trying to say.
She held your hand and took a breath:
"Your father died today."

Mariana Hiotis
*Watertown, NY*

216

# Coming Home

Look to the sky above
In the East…middle east
Sorry, someone's fault I'm late
Year long hold over somewhere
I'm possibly in Kuwait
I'll soon be home, flying mid-air
Look to the sky above
Can you feel a warm breeze
It's all my love coming to
Set you at ease
Together in our hearts
We share the same beat
We hold the same key to
Unlocking our desires to
Be with one another…forever
Our eyes full of tearing
Time is now nearing
Our bodies wanting, burning
Our souls craving & yearning
It's a beautiful day
When I'm on my way
Soon we'll share a happy cry
Look…Look my love at
A gorgeous sky above.

John Morefield
*Louisville, KY*

# The Road to Success

I sort through my thoughts
Good and bad
Bad and good
I notice something quite strange
It scared me a bit
I think of all that could happen
And all that I want to happen
Failure and success
What could hold me back
What could push me forward
The discouragement if frenemies
The encouragement of friends
The hate of haters
And the love of loved ones
But then I stop
Breathe and relax
Because…
Nothing could bring me down
Except for myself
The hate and discouragement of others
Will only make me stronger, wiser, and better
I will not let anyone step in my way
Failure is never an option!

Danielle Taylor
*Dolton, IL*

# Thoughts

Her thoughts are racing,
She must get away.

She walks slowly along the beach,
The shells cold and sharp beneath her feet,
The cool breeze playing havoc with her hair,
The roar of the incoming tide all around her,
The parting of the seagulls as she walks past.

Thoughts of yesterday run through her mind,
Flashes—two people,
Laughing, smiling, holding hands
Them, alone, together

Sadness engulfs her being.
When did it happen?
When did it become them?! Not us!
Was it yesterday, last week, last month,
Last year?  When?!

Now is tomorrow.
Slowly a speck of sun filters thru.
It shadows the dark memories of yesterday.
It's a new beginning, a new start.
It's a new someone to care!

Teresa M. Grandfield
*Melbourne, FL*

# Crossing the Border

Let me help you walk
Old man
Across the border out of
My land

We walk in step
You and I
But our loyalties are
A great divide

I see my father's face
In you
And avert my eyes before
I do
The unthinkable
And care

Gail Madden
*Laurel Springs, NJ*

# Venom

Your slim curvaceous body is sheathed in stunning skin.
With captivating eyes, you lure your prey.
But inside of you, your blood runs icy through your veins
And when you shed your outer shell, I see it's one big flake.

You speak with a forked tongue, but your velvet, coaxing hiss
Entices us to listen to your lies.
Your rumors; your venom, you see the pain you cause
It appears to fuel your power—I see that as a guise.

You bite the hand that feeds you; attack even those who follow you
Feed on weaker targets, what won't put up a fight.
But deep within your heart, you know you're not the strongest
You are a mere con artist with a paralyzing bite.

Once I watched your eyes as you slithered through a field
They locked in upon a harmless, tiny mole.
Your next victim grew larger in those black, reflective slits
And before she even noticed you, you swallowed her up whole.

Insidious creature, vain and proud, you claim to have it all,
Yet few others yearn to seize your throne,
For while you slither on the ground you will never stand tall.
Aside from fleeting followers you will always hunt alone.

Samantha Braun
*Haddonfield, NJ*

## Coffee in Cortez

The days are unknown for their title and purpose
I've sipped coffee in cortez and nothing is the same
Single thoughts of my freedom bring tears
and my loneliness
fades to nothing
self can rest in self
however many a detail may escape
coffee in cortez
waits
unknown dark depths of muggy soul in hand
palms clasp to cup the self
and offer what all we can
a good conversation
a timeless easy feeling
life
coffee in cortez
a morning toast to all creation
a swig from the flask of the Jesus
our sober stagger
stoned by sweet reality
struck and left
coffee in cortez
a long ride yes with only the silent response of the wind
my promise
you will see me again
for coffee in cortez

Rhett Bryan
*Stillwater, OK*

This poem is a verse written during a two-month motorcycle tour of America. I rode an '84 Honda Goldwing named Entity for a total of 14,000 miles from coast to coast and captured my journey in a collection of prose I call Poets Road. Music for "Coffee in Cortez" written and performed by Spoonholster.

## Untitled

When things don't go to suit you,
And the world seems upside down
Don't waste your time in fretting
But drive away that frown and put on a smile
Since life is of perplexing,
'Tis much the widest plan
To bear all trials bravely
And laugh whenever you can

Let us be cheerful
Light-hearted and at peace
You'll find it the very best plan
Jesus will make your path brighter
And make your heart lighter
To laugh whenever you can!

Nakeshia Barnes
*Arcadia, LA*

# Do Own Me!

O Lord! I surrender myself to Thee,
Be my Master and the sole Owner
For now forever of me

Let my heart be filled
With love, devotion and dedication instilled.

My tongue sings your praise and says
Words that soothe people's heart
Bring pleasure for all big and short.

Provide me with ears that listen to
Your admirations, commendations, and acclamation
And hear the voice of people's heart with great perseverance.

Decorate my face with your smile
Grace, soberness and unmatching style.

Give me the hands that caress humanity
Feed people and serve them with humility.

Fill my eyes with kindness, love and forgivefulness,
For all who missed You or are still in wilderness.

Impart me the feet that always step
Towards You constantly, consistently and boldly.
Be always with me in my life, death and through eternity.

Mahesh P. Gupta
*Indianapolis, IN*

## Mona Lisa's Last Day of Posing

I'm late again. He seems annoyed with me,
impatient too. He rants about the light
fading away, having to be just right.
I'm fading too. What does he want to see?

He's struggling with my mouth: how it should be.
"Don't laugh" he says. I frown with all my might.
"No, no" he shouts. How rude and impolite
he is, I dare not say. I need the fee.

Each day he asks that I remove my clothes
then dresses me in heavy frock and shawl
like married women wear when they go out.
A "proper lady" look, I should suppose
and me a prostitute will fool them all.
Now that's a fact I'd almost smile about.

Jane Logan
*Sparks, NV*

# Waiting for a Warm Bus

It is winter. She sits on a bench,
black scarf consuming pale cheeks,
in a battle against wind as it fights to siphon off pink tints;
a tingle the only sign of a hurried onslaughts.

What does she think of? This woman in black,
her puzzler topped with soft snowing gray strands,
whisked every which way, wishing to whirl
with the freedom of those crisp dead things that seem to soar—
dark angels shining against a world of white.

She thinks of all there is to do.
Eager to check her watch, but unwilling to wake
the woolen sleeve as it snuggles sleepily into the cuff of her glove.

She curses the bus driver.
Wonders if he has simply abandoned his post
to sled down an arching slope like that one
that stares at her from across the frozen asphalt.

Or maybe she thinks about those gray strands.
Dancing along her head, ecstatic with energy she no longer exhibits.
Ponders how many more buses she will wait for,
how many more things there will be to do before her own watch dies
and she can drift freely like the leaves;
twirl on tingling toes as she whispers to the winter traveler
sitting on a bench in a warm woolen scarf
just thinking about how cold it is on the lonely corner.

Kristie A. Schlauraff
*East Moriches, NY*

# Day by Day

Day by day, night by night,
I hide under my blanket, trembling with fright.
Night by night, day by day,
Wondering if awake I should stay.
Day by night, night by day;
Wondering if I shall yell, "Hey" to my mom, "Hey" to my pop.
As soon as I know it my bed starts to drop,
Through a trapdoor
I was screaming with fright.
When the bed finally stopped, it was night.
I could see the sun shining through my glass door.
I jumped off my bed and landed on the floor.
I ran through the hallways and around the bend.
I finally woke up, and that is the end.

So if you're in bed trembling with a fright,
Just remember to buy a night light.

Scout Van Cise
*Saegetown, PA*

## Little Hands

His hands reach up, she's filled with joy
…Mommy's little boy
Passing football, getting muddy
…Daddy's little buddy

Baking cookies, riding bikes
Outgrown pj's, hugs goodnight
Skinned up knees from climbing trees
Milk mustaches, A-B-C's

Little hands to wave "Goodbye"
Messy hair and sleepy eyes
Blowing bubbles, sandbox play
Puddles jumped on rainy days

Toothless smiles, growing feet
Counting stars, "Trick or Treat!"
Pumpkins carved so faces glow
Angels made in winter snow

Morning cartoons, untied laces
Soaring kites, go-cart races
Cars and trucks, building blocks
Hide and seek, mismatched socks

Fishing poles, big green frogs
Skipping stones, fetching dogs,
Lightening bugs in mason jars
Little Hands to Hold in Ours

Debbie Skatula
*St. Clairsville, OH*

# "In Response to William Blake's 'The Tyger' and 'The Lamb'"

Regard the Lamb, wooly white
Grazing most peacefully
Innocent Lamb, the world's Light
Dost thou know who made thee?

Note the tyger, the prowling beast
Who foul and fair entwine
Deceived thy prey, thy Lamb now fleeced
Is he same creator thine?

Could it be thy Immoral Smith,
The Mastor Sculptor would limn
A brute among the Lamb and kith,
Both serpent and seraphim?

Darling Blake, 'tis not thy Smith who moves either to groan
'Tis by choice the Lamb doth graze, and the tyger's will his own.

Shelby B. Butler
*Bossier City, LA*

# You

You open my mind
You open my eyes
You open my heart
That's how you make me feel when
I am around you
I feel so good when
I am around you
I wish this day will never end when
I am around you
You open my thoughts you make me
Express how I feel no one made
Me
Do this besides you I love your smile
I love you enthusiasm I love your caring heart.
It's you I want to be with
Through thick and thin
I thank the woman who raised you
To be a wonderful person such as
You
It's a blessing that God blessed
Me with an Angel
From the skies
Because I finally found you

Gregory Julmice
*Jamaica, NY*

## Secrets

These tears role down my face.
I hate this horrid place.
All the screaming and slamming doors,
I can't take this anymore!
Behind these eyes
Tells no lies for secrets ever more.

Alissa Scrantz
*Las Vegas, NV*

## A Quiet Time

A time when winds are nil…
The cat's asleep…
The sun hides behind low gray clouds…
The television is off…the radio is still…
The hum of the fridge is barely there…
No neighbors chatting in the yard…
The children not yet returned from school…
A quiet time…and yet…
The resounding echo of all the things you've wished
you've done…
And all the dreams that still lie ahead…
Abound in your head louder than a marching band
on the 4th of July.

Barbara Affrunti
*Franklin Square, NY*

## Jacob's Guardian

The old man walked thru the unlit room,
To the crib of his great-grandson,
He stood in the darkness on this cold winter night,
To admire what the "Good Lord" had done.
"Well now" the old man said with a grin,
"Let's have a look at you lad,"
His eyes were aglow as he softly spoke,
"You've got the shoulders and hands of your dad,"
As he studied the child with obvious love,
He cast such a pitful sight,
An old Irishman bent from age and toil,
In the dark of a cold winter's night,
A shot...a shot...
The retort of a gun,
exploded the cold night air,
The whine of a bullet
as it crashed thru the wall,
struck the crib with the child right there,
An instant, a heartbeat, nay, nothing so long,
Did the old man's instincts endure,
His hand shot out with a warrior's speed,
And swept the bullet to the floor,
In the weeks to come men marveled how,
The bullet had dropped in its flight,
But we who knew him have no doubt at all,
Jake met his great-grandpa that night.

David E. McCracken
*Homer City, PA*

We live on a small farm nestled in the hills of Western Pennsylvania. On a December night in 2004 an errant round, fired from a hill above our son's house, crashed through the bedroom wall of our youngest grandson and struck a slat on his crib. What defies logic and baffles experts was the location of the spent round. It should have dropped down or recoiled back. The bullet was found past the foot of the crib. "Almost" as one man said, "as if it was altered by an outside force." You may believe what you will.

# Open Arms

It's not something to be tampered with,
messed with or destroyed.
It can make a man, or kill a man,
or leave him in between.
The power of it lies within your hands, you're free to come and go,
use it wisely, and you will know;
That this feeling cannot be abused, rented or borrowed,
it's there whenever you need it,
not whenever you want it.
This feeling never lies, it's always sincere,
it's as real as burning your tongue on an un-cooled cup of tea.
It is confusing yes,
but in the end it's best,
to feel this love,
a true test.
Love is worth living for,
without it life's a joke, it's what we all wake up for,
and we always want some more.
Everyone needs love in life,
so live it with open arms,
always keep your heart warm,
and in the end you'll see,
loving somebody truly,
is the best that you can be.

Brandon Mouery
*Harrisburg, PA*

## Burning Roses

Burning roses to hide my pain.
Understand what I mean.
Remember all the treasured times.
Notice what they mean.
Impossible to realize my pain.
Nothing can revive me from the pain I resign.
Growing stronger, my emotions extend.
Realize the good and forget the bad.
Open your eyes and visualize your dreams.
Speak your thoughts and you'll be heard.
Express your feeling and you will be remembered.
Sing your heart out and be revived forever.

Tiffany DeGarmo
*Newberg, OR*

My poem was inspired by the music type of Evanescence. I really enjoy entering poetry competitiions. My parents are very proud of the poetry I write. I want to thank everyone for reading my poem.

# Now

Pages turn
calendars burn
decades gone before I blink.
Capture the moment,
childhood bliss,
the treasure in a baby's kiss.
Look to the future,
plant your soul,
in the depth
of a love lived whole.
Savor the past,
give kindness away,
Now, before
death demands its toll.

Lee Ann Swick
*Columbus, OH*

## To Life

There are choices we make,
There are chances we take,
Is it what life is all about?

There are friends we love,
There are enemies we hate,
Is it what life is all about?

From childhood on we wonder,
What happens to those who blunder?
They who always look to make excuses,
To demean life with false abuses.

So we stand proud of ourselves
And our accomplishments,
Or do we fear why
We lack confidence?

No matter what we think,
Say, or aspire to do,
There will always be something
To challenge us from out of the blue.

So let us toast to the fact
We made it this far,
Let us toast to the heavens,
And reach for that star,

Lets us toast to love,
To peace, to eternity…"To Life."

William Dratler
*Miami Beach, FL*

# The Lake

The lake is so peaceful, so quiet, so calm
the loon likes to holler in the morning sun
You can't quite tell when the morning is done
the fish keep on jumping for flies and for bugs
The morning's so bright, so peaceful, so calm
the boats are all docked except for one
The dogs are all sleeping, the tools put away
the bats are all tired from their nightly parade
When the morning is done, everyone is awake
then we come in from the lake.

Ryan J. Reagan
*Burnsville, MN*

# Beloved Poems

A novel once read, once lived.
A story told, a tale known.
Ah…but a poem!
Words on a page
To be read again and again.
Ingested
Ever
So
Slowly,
With passion and fervor in thought,
Your poems are the prelude to sensorial form.

Chrissie H. Birben
*Yaphank, NY*

# Grandpa

My best friend, my best pal
You should know—it's my Grandpa Al.
He always jokes around with me,
Tells funny stories and we watch TV.
The animal shows, the Price is Right,
He loved snacks and candies and sweets
And always said, "Hey kid! Want a treat?"
I helped push him to church in his wheelchair each week,
Until his body became too weak.
Then I sat by his bed and talked and talked
Since he could no longer walk.
When he got too sick to talk to me,
I prayed to the angels to come and let him rest in peace.
I cried and cried because I didn't want to let him go,
But I knew God was calling him to go home,
God needed a good, fun-loving soul up there,
And God knew just the man.
My best friend was my Grandpa Al—
Everyone should be lucky enough to have such a great pal.

Erik Geiman
*Ft. Thomas, KY*

My poem was written on the day of my grandpa's funeral. I am the youngest of five kids and the only boy besides my father. My mom is a nurse. My grandfather and I were best buds. My mom quit her job to take care of my grandpa and I assisted her. Grandpa was kind, funny, and liked to joke around, he was also very religious. He became very ill and died. I will never forget all my fun days and good memories with him. I am glad I was able to help take care of him.

238

# What Is a Friend?

A friend is someone who doesn't come in any size, color or shape
A friend is a loving caring person who knows how to relate
A friend is someone who would never turn their back on you
No matter how hard the situation may be, a friend will see you make it
through
A friend will cry when you cry and laugh when you laugh
A friend will never hesitate to do whatever you ask
A friend is someone you can tell anything to
A friend is that special someone that will never deceive you
A friend won't pierce you in your back or tear your character down
A friend can definitely be trusted when your companion is around
When friends have disagreements, there is never any love lost
A friend will go the distance for you at any cost
So ask yourself, "Am I really that true friend
That will remain loyal to that person until the very end?"

Starlene R. Patterson
*New York, NY*

I wrote this poem during a part of my life where I was incarcerated for eight years in
Federal Prison for something that I did. I was evaluating the relationships that I had with
people whom I considered friends before and during this trial in my life and I was also
questioning myself to see if I was indeed a friend to them. In the end, I knew I was a
friend but many of them were not.

# From the Heart

She scampers away when I come around.
She tries to get away quickly without even a sound.
I try to say hello, I try to be polite.
Still, she looks at me as if I would bite.
She seems to think I hate her with all of my heart,
That if given the chance I would tear her apart.
I was puzzled when I first saw her reaction to me.
Then suddenly it became very clear to see.
It's not that I'm scary, frightening, mean or unkind.
It' because she feels jealousy is first on my mind.
What things she must have been told baffle me yet,
For she had an odd view of me even before we had met.
It feels strange to be seen as a threat or competition.
Yet, flattering to be seen worthy of such a position.
You see, she loves the man who used to love me,
And I love the boy that she will never see.
For in our youth we shared first love, even a first kiss.
My sweet boy that time stole I will always miss.
Was I just a butterfly swooned over with childish glee,
And is she his forever sweet just like a honeybee?
First love is forever and true love will never die.
Yet, when they marry as planned, I fear I will cry.
Still, as long as he's happy and pursuing what's right,
Then I can be content and not put up a fight.

Vanessa Carruth
*N. Granville, NY*

## To Brookie

"Granddaughter of ours, on your "Special Day"
We're here with you in Spirit, our thoughts sent your way.
You're lovely as a picture, we see you're doing swell.
This new addition to your heart, we trust he'll treat you well.

We see all the excitement that's going on down there,
The planning, the flowers, the laughter of Grandkids fair
Oh yes, we see that little blonde, we think she's one of ours,
The one with the little basket, dropping all the flowers

And now as we think of memories past, We see another child,
Left school one day for Grandma's house, was only 'bout a mile.
She saw no danger at the age of five, 'Our Home' was her world,
You do remember, don't you Brooke, you were that little girl.

And as you start your life together, our hope is in your choice,
Be still and listen and you will hear, that quiet and gentle voice.
He'll teach you all you need to know, in "Him" you can confide,
There's nothing more important than making "Him" your guide.

Well now you're all grown up, and you have your life to live.
So live it to its fullest, be gracious…To others give.
Have love and understanding, just remember, don't be late,
Granddaddy and I will be waiting…we'll meet you at the gate."

Carol Williams
*Pace, FL*

I guess I am not very versed on poetry, but I have written a lot of songs. My husband and I have two children and six grandchildren. I wrote the poem "To Brookie" for my niece, who was getting married at the time. We are a very close-knit family and she has always wanted my parents to be at her wedding. I am sorry to say they both had passed away by the time the wedding day came. The poem was to inspire her and to let her know that they were there in spirit.

## Love's Bouquet

Little ones, precious ones,
An answer to a prayer
Looking at your faces
Tells us God is there.

Smiling at your mother,
Laughing with your dad,
All the world can see that
You're the best they could have had.

See Colette, angelic,
And Lauren, fair and sweet.
Next is gentle Graham,
then Nicholaus, oh, so neat.

Boys and girls and toys and curls,
Happy days together.
Laughing, crying, playing, sighing
In every kind of weather.

You are Sunday's children
Born on Father's Day.
Nestled all together
Making a bouquet.

As you grow together
May you grow in grace.
Brother, sister, sister, brother
None can take your place.

Elizabeth A. Tonner
*Rensselaer, IN*

One June 15, 1997, Father's Day, our son, Christopher Tonner, received the ultimate gift from his wife, Julie. It was a beautiful bouquet of babies named Colette, Graham, Nicholaus, and Lauren. Who could not pen words of love concerning this spectacular event?! After appearing in a segment of 20/20 with these darlings this grandmother had to try. I have been an aspiring poet for ten years and try to capture all the main events in my family's lives—my husband, four sons and one daughter, their spouses plus seventeen grandchildren. Words convey so much. My poetry is part of me.

# My Mom Is a Wave

Bringing in good and gentle
Things,
In the morning she comes in as a
Gentle tide
Like a calm and cool day
And I wake up to a gentle rocking
She then gets me out of bed
And brings me what I need
When she helps me
She gives me a warm feeling
Inside
Like she always does
And cares for me when I'm sick
She guides me through life
And, my mom is a wave

Tyler Loeding
*Lexington, MI*

## The 65-Year-Old Blues

I'll miss the bounce of my youthful step
And my flowing natural brown hair
I'll miss the days of mini-skirts
When I'd let my legs go bare.

Goodbye, goodbye to chocolate éclairs,
I'll remember what you did:
To make me smile, to give me cheer,
Since I was just a kid.
To add 10 lbs…but make me smile,
Since I was just a kid.

I'll miss the days before Medicare
And my orthopedic shoes
I'll miss my mind probably most of all.
I've got the 65-year-old blues.

So goodbye, goodbye to all those things
I'll remember what I had.
Just looking now at family and friends
My life didn't turn out so bad.

I'm resigned to this age and I'm a winner
And tonight I'll have dessert BEFORE dinner!

Phyllis C. Altopp
*Cleveland, TN*

# Act of Tradition

Each year visitors would be less
We look back and we must confess
They were great times for the queen
She worked endlessly to make it a happy scene.


She would never let them leave with an empty hand,
This made her happy and in time we would understand.
Each year we wanted her to do less and less,
With our help, there was more of a mess.

She was tired but happy with our act of good intent,
After all, we were there to carry on the event.
She is no longer there to smooth out the mess,
Each year we carry on, but with one less.

Al Juliano
*Warwick, NY*

## What a Wonderful Life

What a wonderful life we have here on earth
We sing, we play, and we work
At times life seems unfair
But we know God will be there
He helps us through it all
Every day, even when night falls
He watches over us with a steady hand
Like a Shepherd and his sheep
We should thank Him
For all His help

Yet when you misbehave
God is slow to anger
How nice is He for making us who we are today
If we love God and we appreciate Him
Like we always should
And we want to thank Him
That is when we
Pray

Cara M. Mills
*Summerfield, NC*

I think what inspires me to write poetry is my family. I had my share of doubts too, but my family is always there to help me through it. My Nana is the one who encourages me to enter competitions.

## Like It Was Yesterday

I remember like it was yesterday. We had just come in off patrol
I'd slipped my wet boots off, and was rubbing some blood up to my toes.
When I noticed Smitty shiver and let out a muffled moan
And I knew right then and there that Smitty was going home alone.

I remember like it was yesterday, another time, another place.
We were flying tight formation with Messerschmitts right in our face.
I saw my Wingman's cockpit shatter and watched as the plane went down.
I cried, as no chute opened as the B-17 hit the ground.

I remember like it was yesterday and I was just a kid in a place we called Pearl
It was 1941 and I fresh off the farm and out to see the world.
I watched the plane come diving down and saw the bombs fall.
Then the Arizona became a flaming tomb and I lost my two best Friends.

I remember like it was yesterday, but I don't know when or even where.
There was peace on Earth—There was no war, No weapons of mass
destruction could be found anywhere.
Then I saw the Great Commander… He said. "The victory is finally won."
And to veterans of all the ages, "Well done, my good and faithful sons."

Bill Jewell
*Henderson, TN*

## Car Seats

Two empty car seats set in the back of my mind
And nobody knows the love of a father—this day in time.
How could she do this—oh God you know it's not fair.
How come it feels like I'm the only one who cares?
Tears in their eyes and mine just won't stop—and time doesn't
heal this wound of mine.
And two empty car seats set in the back of my mind.

Now the phone's been disconnected and she don't seem to care—
It's just part of her way and now I can't talk to or hear the two
boys I once held dear. Oh God I care—don't let them
think I don't—They're getting older and I feel like I'm running out of
time.
And two empty car seats set in the back of my mind.

I missed their first snow—we never get any down here.
I missed a lot of things—oh God I'm so scared I wonder what
they're doing each and every day I'm not there. I want to be a father
I really do care.
But nobody seems to know how a father feels this day in time.
And two empty car seats set in the back of my mind.

They're in my heart and that's where they will always be.
I do my best but I know that it's just not enough. I know life
can be hard but I never thought it could be so tough.
My boys need their father and their father needs his boys and
I pray that one day everything will be fine—but until then—
Two empty car seats set in the back of my mind.

Jeffery C. Stadalis
*Bay St. Louis, MS*

## Chistmas Is About

Christmas is about joys,
Not about toys
Christmas is about the love and laughs,
Not about people with cookies, who give noogies
Christmas is about turkey,
Not beef jerky you buy at the corner store
Christmas is about sitting around the table
Not sitting in a playpen eating lint out of your navel
Christmas is about reading a book near the nook,
Not picking gum out from under the table,
Where people look and read fable
Christmas is about telling Jesus' story
Not reading fables you found at the table
Christmas is about decorating a tree,
Not burnin' the tree
Christmas is about drinking eggnog,
Not about watching a hedgehog in the dirt.

Aly Bass
*Dadeville, AL*

# The Pastor

This is God's number one son
He praises every Sunday and cannot let his work go undone
The most lovable man of the church
He whips Jesus into people's hearts but not like a birch
With a strong tone he delivers the word
With stories no one ever heard
The songs he sings are so fruitful
It makes everyone's soul feel useful
On holidays the church always gives to the needy
But all the homeless just get a little too greedy
He likes to hold intelligent conversations
And meet new people from all over the nations
The older women love to scream and shout
They love their pastor without a doubt
He is an honorable trustworthy man
And a loving husband to his beautiful wife, Joanne
Dresses in the finest clothes
But how he gets them no one knows
He wears a lot of jewelry that matches his eyes
But everything he started to say was a lie
Could be stealing and could be creeping
He is not lying in his bed so where is he sleeping
Joanne wonders could it be me
And little did she know that it was a he

Nicole Gibson
*Pikesville, MD*

## Untitled

I must confess that my house is a mess.
Cleaning is not my strongest cup of tea.
My world, some may say, is in total disarray
Nothing personal mind you, it's just me!

I haven't washed clothes since God only knows,
Nor the dishes nor toilet nor even the sink
That reminds me by the way, I missed garbage day!
But, it's quite OK, I'm immune to the stink.

Dust bunnies pounce and play all day
And roam peacefully about the place,
but by night the parasites and dust mites fight
over squatter's rights to my pillowcase.

I really don't care, if my walls need repair,
and I could not tell you for certain.
Though ridden with cracks, both forward and back
They're all hidden, behind cobweb curtains.

Clothes are strewn throughout each room,
So are my bottles, my books and my bike.
My socks all resemble snowflakes,
because there are no two alike.

I consider it my job, being a slob,
the fact that I'm good, cannot be denied.
So, I'll just leave things the way they are,
meanwhile, let's just stay outside.

Dave Anderson
*Clarkston, MI*

# Death

Death is not anything,
I'm only passing to the other side.
I am me, you are you.
This that I was for you, I will always be.

Give me the name that you always gave me,
Speak to me as you always have done.
Do not use it any differently.
Do not take a solemn air or be sad.

Continue to laugh the laugh
That we laughed together,
That my name be known in the house,
Like it always has been.

Without pompousness or anything of the kind,
Without a trace of shadow
Life means all this, which has always been.
The thread is not cut.

Why would I be out of your thoughts,
Because I am out of your view
I am not far...
Just on the other side of the road.

Odle Davis
*Iuka, MS*

# The Last Run

A cloudless day with sky so clear
What a beautiful day for a run
Through the sun-drenched streets I have no fear
I've always thought it quite fun.
I Lace up my shoes and get ready to run
I can think about things troubling me
Four miles today & all in the sun
And I know it will set my mind free.
Today I ask Jesus to run with me
So we can talk man to man and be frank
He's always willing and will always be
That fact you can take to the bank.
Forgive me, Lord, for my sins you've seen
I ask as we run stride for stride
He says "your sins are already known & washed clean"
"From Me you know you can't hide."
We continue to run and the miles go by
It seems like longer than four
One more thing, Lord, when it's my turn to die
I want to come home through Your door.
He smiled and said, "do not fret"
"Your place is waiting for free"
"Your time is coming, but not quite yet"
"Keep running & talking to Me."
So we run some more & talk when we can
I guess what I'm asking today
Did I do good in life, was I a good man?
My heart swelled when He said, "you're okay"
We finished our run and sat down to rest
Then He said with a loving smile
"My son, you've done well & passed every test"
"Your race is done, you've run your last mile."
He said, "I welcome you home in the winner's lane
Now you can rest and be free"
"In Heaven there's no sorrow, no hurt, & no pain
And thank you for running with Me."

Robert E. Larson
*Grinnell, IA*

253

# A Happy Birthday to Cliff

In these beautiful aesthetic surroundings
Celebrating eighty years of Cliff's life,
We see God's goodness shown through him;
Enhanced by a loving supportive wife.

He never found that 'rocking chair'
We doubt he ever looked for one;
His multifaceted ministries include
Sharing musical talents, plus just having fun.

Many would be the memories of those he knew
During those years of pastoral ministry,
Plus Warren Memorial Hospital connections
Who benefited from his role of Chaplaincy.

While an accomplished pastor, teacher, musician—
His humble spirit also comes through;
While he would shun showered accolades
We feel some recognition is due.

So here is to Cliff Walton, friend to many;
Young at heart, that is also a known fact—
Keep that warm smile active
And that vibrant sense of humor intact.

May your birthday and the years to come
Bring many blessings from on high—
Adding more special memories
As each year to come passes by.

You are loved!

Doris M. Anderson
*Warren, PA*

At age ten my attention was drawn to a row of spindly birch trees in our family backyard. The morning's mail included Joyce Kilmers's poem "Trees;" started writing poems at that point. Occasionally a book of poems would mysteriously appear on my bed. My mother broadened my interest when she'd quote Rudyard Kipling: "We would love each other better if we only understood." This, when I or a sibling voiced a criticism of someone else. The future included a career in India where that poem changed my western outlook, learning to see others more realistically.

# A Legend in Our Time

To hear him talk, the way he thinks, you know he is a kitten,
But on the field, or the bench, the legend's being written.
He's been here since time began, he is a giant of a man.
Great recognition, he gets none, but he's the cause the game is won.
He has a mighty bat it's true, he has an awesome swing, the wind, the
pitch, a drive to
right, he makes the bleachers ring.
The upper decks are full you see of marks he has achieved.  They build
new parks, he
tears them down, he's not to be believed.
He is the Captain of our team, a legend in our town, His mind is always
on the game, and
still has time to clown around.
The Captain swings and Milo screams "the ball is outta sight," another
game is in the books, he's won for us this night.
When No. 8 steps to the plate, the pitcher's stomach quivers, they
challenge him with blinding speed, but still the man delivers.
I guess I could go on for days, and talk about the many ways, he makes
the Pirates shine,
But I will close and watch in awe,
"A LEGEND IN OUR TIME"

Frank Certo
*N. Cambria, PA*

255

# Probably

As we sit in our
polished pews
singing softly "Silent Night"
we sometimes tend to forget
the reality behind Christmas
Mary in all probability
needed a bath
And Jesus was lying in straw
that probably contained lice
And Joseph was being tormented
by nightmares and daydreams
and probably
other quite logical fears
like how to pay the taxes again this year
And why is it that
the glitter and gaud
of our twentieth century Christmas
Cannot compare to one very bright star…
Bring us back Lord to the reality of a Savior
Born in a manger
Bound for a cross
and with all probabilities laid aside
we will discover the secret
behind that
very bright
Star.

Linda Aiken
*Cochrnton, PA*

# Before the Leaves Fall

The most colorful and beautiful time of all
Is early in the fall season before the leaves fall
The sun overhead now shines forth her light
That colors the sky what a beautiful sight
As I see the valleys below all filled with dew
And all the mountains and trees what a magnificent view
As the rays of the sun now shine on the trees
The leaves begin to fall without even a breeze
The old leaves fall down to make room for quite a few
That come early in springtime shining green and new
Of all the beauty below and all the colors above
Could only be given by the hand of God's love
Who loved us enough He was willing to go
Down to this earth so everyone may know
That life eternal is theirs if they only believe
In the finished work of Christ on the cross of Calvary

Catherine Myers
*Spring Grove, PA*

# Owed to the Credit Card Companies

I've spent my money by the yard
Charged it to my credit card.
When those debts I had to cover
Charged them to the card Discover.

I didn't leave home without the Master
Now I have a real disaster.
The interest mushroomed to the sky;
Yes, it's past a real good cry.

Oh, I spent a lot of money
On a gorgeous Playboy bunny;
Diamonds, trips and fancy bars,
Casinos, travels, imported cars.

Visa, Master, will not relent
They demand their big percent.
Oh yes, the bills are overdue
And now I've met my Waterloo.

So off I go to the County jail,
No credit left to pay the bail.
The repo man—he doesn't care,
Stripped me down to my underwear.

One sad lesson I had to learn,
Never spend until you earn.
The Bill Collector has surely won
And this poem, like me, is done!

William Breisacher
*Pennsauken, NJ*

# Kids

Some kids are mean
Some kids are nice
And believe me I know what it's like
I have brothers and sisters of my own
First they began to crawl then they began to walk
Then they began to talk back
That's the tough part
I know they cried
I know sometimes they smell funny
But you know they can laugh too…
Even with you
Even though sometimes they can be a pain
Well…
This is what I always say…
You gotta love 'em

Chris Parkhurst
*Toledo, WA*

# Mirror, Mirror

Mirror, mirror on the wall,
who's the greatest actor of them all?
Parading around with a smile on my face,
hiding my pain and waiting for it to erase.

But the mirror knows, it's my worst enemy,
it's the other side of me.
Seeing truth, it shatters my mask,
Cutting so much that I don't even have to ask...

Mirror, mirror on the wall,
will you smile when I finally fall?

Brett Butler
*Rockland, ME*

# The Master Plan

In this modern world of ours,
Empiricism rules;
Skeptics feel that God is just
An opiate for fools!

If it can't be measured,
It's much like the "Holy Grail."
Causing an elusive search—
A child-like fairytale.

Well, please excuse my foolishness
Or lack of common sense,
In thinking that our world could not
Evolve from nothingness!

Galaxies speak volumes
Of God's handiwork above,
While sunset hues and patterns
Testify to His great love.

Mountain peaks and oceans deep
Exhort His name on high;
Design without Designer, though,
Does common sense defy!!

While faith can be elusive,
It's a quest on which we roam;
I know mine will sustain me
'Til my savior calls me home.

Louise M. Heaberlin-Goff
*Vail, AZ*

# The Leaves

Thank you Lord...for the seasons
Thank you for the fall,
Thank you for the colored leaves
and the beauty of it all.
As I sit here and watch
the leaves raining down,
I'm amazed at the beauty
they spread all around.
A once barren land,
now brightly colored ground.
And then...as I look...
at a nearly naked tree,
somewhat drab and plain to see,
I think...it's a lot like you and me.
For it's not what we wear
or who we might be,
but what's inside and what we share,
that gives us real beauty.
So I hope Lord...when it's time
For my leaves to fall,
that they spread joy and kindness
to one and to all.
So others might then,
be able to see,
the beauty and love,
You have shown me.

Gary A. Schuetz
*Wausau, WI*

# Life's Drips

Drip…drip…drip…
Look at life's faucet
It's flow has slowly been turning off.
Drip…drip…drip…
The melancholy dreams on.
Close your eyes
Let life's drama play on.
Childhood nestled in time
Favorite things and hobbies
Settle themselves into day-to-day living.
Drip…drip…drip…
Adolescence moves into young adulthood
Pressures and questions flood the mind
Who am I?  What do I want to become?
Drip…drip…drip…
Adulthood, a time to explore ideas
Try on passing and permanent relationships
Wander along avenues of thought and action
Only to discover that the lines and wrinkles
Of life and body have caught up?

Yet, if the faucet of life
Is turned on just a little more
The bowl of life fills up with goals fulfilled,
Dreams achieved, and, yes, HOPE LIVES ON!

Carol Chupick
*Sterling Heights, MI*

# What a Weary Day

Cold is the day, happy am I!
Mighty in Passion and in Fear
No boundaries to adhere.

High spirits was her game
But I'll never play to blame
Wanting it must be, supplicating me

No More, I said
Your border has no thread
Standing there, she beheld my face
Regret and sorrow filled her stead

Slowly stepped out through the door
A shrieking sound to behold
Stunned she was, but she was cold
And could not disperse from her hold

Screaming! Shouting! Skuffling!
Rescue! Help! But unable to behold
Peace and calm came to her head
Which was all over in dredge

Minutes! All over! It was done!
Silver cuffs glittered embraced their hands
Sorry! But it was over
The deed was done
ALAS! The deed was done

Bernadette G. de Gouvier
*Ft. Myers, FL*

## The Daisy

Sun's navel
encircled by eagerly
outstretched receptors
of chaste white

perceiving nature's offerings:
morning dewdrops, cool shadows
of passing clouds, cricket tones,

neighboring blades of grass
conversing of meadow happenings,
the crossing of an uneasy cottontail
who stops to munch some clover.

But wait. A biped's vibrations
are coming closer—
a child bewitched by the daisy's
disposition smiles
leans over, picks it
and carefully braids
it into her hair.

Diana Gomez
*Pittsfield, MA*

# Untitled

I sit here on the doorstep
Waiting for you right here
Waiting for you for years and years
And when you finally come
I'd like you to hear these words
Words just a few
That I scribbled down
Just for you
I'll play you my heart
All over my guitar
I'll sing you a song so softly
That you'll move closer to hear
I'll hold on forever
Baby never say never
Your second home is my heart
So for love don't look far
Every day I find happiness
It's always in your words and smile
So stay longer, just for this little while
Your voice so far away in the distance
But I can feel it
An endless nothing separates us
Leaves us in silence
And I hate that silence

Dan Beckley
*Sunderland, MA*

# Graffiti

Words written in a cave, upon a wall of stone
Eons and eons age, where someone once called home…
Ancient times .. Ancient tools .. Ancient man .. Ancient ways ..
Still yet, Ancient man had words to say…
"Ancient Graffiti"

Words written in the sand…
Silent words, for whom to understand?
Catch it quick! What did it say?..
Before foamy waters, forever, wash away.
"Sandy Beach Graffiti"

Words written upon a wall…
Literary evidence—A silent voice of call.
Words escaping from mind to hand…
For unsuspecting eyes, and mind, to understand.
"Wall Graffiti"

Billboards along the highway…
Catching the motorists' eyes…
Flashing bits of commercial wares…
Just tempting you to buy!
"Commercial Graffiti"

Initials carved into a tree…
A lover's wish for the other to see.
The tree still stands, old and tall…
Did the love hold true … through the years … through it all?
"A Lover's Graffiti"

Thomas Marlow
*Louisville, KY*

# Twelve Months

It started with a magical, midnight kiss
at the beginning of a fresh New Year.
By the time Valentine's Day came around
cupid's arrows hearts had speared.
When spring had sprung, and all was green,
to each other they were "dear."
Easter's hunt found treasure, (in an egg)
an engagement ring appeared.
Their romance grew and blossomed
as their wedding day did near.
Then that special, summer day, in June…
at their wedding, all eyes teared.
Kisses and caresses cause fireworks,
as he softly whispers in her ear.
Sultry summer days spent tanning…
bodies with aromatic oils smeared.
Cool autumn nights for star gazing
at the evening skies…crystal clear.
October brings all Hallow Eve…
With him, not a thing is feared.
They offer thanks for taking two
and molding one…forever to endear.
Their first Christmas they praise the Lord for his
fluted glasses raised…togetherness they cheer.

Niki Dempsey
*Hatfield, AR*

# Shari

At what point does the disease take over
And you become the cancer
The minority in your own body

I can't be the man in this situation
I can't be the man
The rock
The provider
The man

And I barely even knew you
Imagine if I did
Imagine if I didn't

Then I could be the man
The fake
The pretender
The man

Clayson Lobb
*Winchester, IL*

## You Asked

You asked me what I'm thinking
but this I cannot tell
you asked me and the truth is
it makes me want to yell.

I have no right to feel like this
to another you are wed.
But the way I feel about you, well...
I musta bumped my head.

If I told you what I truly feel
I think you'd run like hell
For you belong to someone else
and my heart I tried to tell.

I'd love to let you know
why I feel so blue.
But, so far I have no right
to tell you I love you!

Stephanie Tamayo
*Sallisaw, OK*

# Heavy Sleeper

You close your eyes in pain,
And pull up the sheets for comfort.
You find yourself asleep,
But you don't really care.
You actually think it helps,
And you wish it so always:
Never worrying about problems,
No more enduring pain;
Time seems to soar away as
Seconds become minutes, and
The minutes soon are hours.
Before you have realized it,
You've slept the day away.
But then you start to wonder,
"Should I really live my life as so?
Forget everything, and rely on my dreams?"
The days have become weeks…
And soon, you've slept for years.
You can't recall the face in the mirror.
'Cause you've slept through life
To escape from your pain…
But, in conclusion…
You've missed your chance for joy.

Nathan Davis
*Louisville, KY*

# The Pill Age

How many pills does it take to keep you feeling well?
As you get older are you like me?  That number seems to swell.
Pills become a way of life.  It's just a matter of when.
Every time our "parts" go out another pill goes in. My calendar now is
loaded but not one social date.
Doctor appointments I must keep where I always have to wait.
Many others wait there too, a blank look on each face.
Time seems to be suspended as we sit and stare in space.
How good it is to hear my name and I exit from this gloom,
But now I have to wait again…it's just a smaller room.
As I wait I often think how good I used to feel.
A pill was something others took but now it's with each meal.
When at last I'm on my way with help for current ills,
I head for home but not before I stop and buy more pills.

Don White
*Shelbyville, KY*

# Fall

Fall comes with his cool breath
and flirty breeze—such a tease!
Geese pinned like medals on his sky-breast
to boast of Summer's conquest.
Fall, sharp dressed man, tucks in his sun.
Before he dons cool night shades
he winks at me with a cloudy eye
and stirs a cricket serenade
so that I will linger
in his ephemeral embrace.

Dana M. Martin
*Louisville, KY*

Dana resides in the river city Louisville, Kentucky. She recently earned two masters degrees with honors and looks forward to teaching university courses. She has penned poetry since 1970 and plans to publish a compilation. Her poetry often reflects her philosophies that "life is art" and "it's all an adventure!" She shares this rich adventure with all who touch her.

## Freedom Bells

Freedom bells ring out
false news
Death count goes up
no agreements pursued
Political powers pointless
if they can't speak the truth
Nothing really changes
just the daily news
tragic is the same old story
told every two hours
till its squeezed of its juice
Freedom bells ring out
bringing us false news
Politicians keep us blinded
from the real truth
We the people need remind
them we're loving proof
what's their excuse.

Brett Reckelhoff
*Ontario, CA*

## Night Stalker

He creeps up on you—
He preys on you—
He eats away at your soul—

He takes every ounce of life
From your body—

He replaces it with Gloom, Despair—
A sense of Death that on one sees—
Of Hopelessness that no one feels—
Of Despair that no one cares—

The night stalker—
He creeps up silent—
He creeps up cold—
He comes alone—
To take with him your very soul—

The Night Stalker
He will be your Friend
Till the very end

Cindy Creech
*Richmond, IN*

# Epitaph

Sitting on the hardest rock
The world has ever known
All alone, I'm by myself
With all my hair wind blown
I wonder how I got here
I'm not sure where I've been
I only know that when I knocked
They wouldn't let me in
Thinking mostly of the past
I try to figure out
Why optimism went away
And made me live in doubt
This isn't what I hoped for
It's sure not what I want
In front of me there's more hard rocks
I know I must confront
They may be hard as metal
But not as tough as me
I plan to crush them into dust
A total victory

George K. Bruno
*Lomita, CA*

# Beauty for a Word

It is far deeper than we see
It attracts us, devotes us and detains us
for it is only a word
We use it so common yet so unaware
and still we wonder why we use it
for it is only a word
Speak for only good
for never sad
for it is only a word
It will capture the strongest of us
It will break the fear of us
for it is only a word
Feeling for another is more than a word
It is a true bond of thoughts to feeling
and thoughts to feeling are of your making
Sincerity is my making
and beauty to me is far more than a word.

Anthony R. Miller
*Mobile, AL*

# Adrift

Like a fallen leaf on a forgotten pond, floating aimlessly
With nowhere to go but down.
Once a brilliant and vibrant part of something better.
Belonging, yet knowing that one day it must end
with the autumn season's wind.
And so it comes to pass, as I was drifting on that breeze of life,
a whirlwind of commotion, chaotic, endless strife,
When a stranger reached down and lifted me up.
She saw something that made the others
Just keep walking on by—
And suddenly the winds blew a little warmer,
the rains fell a little gentler,
The color, the vibrancy and the life returned.
And with that a beautiful new season began.
As a young woman and her man
embark on a wondrous new journey together
To soar on the summer breeze forever.

Timothy Fournier
*Malone, NY*

The inspiration for this poem came as I realized that our twenty-fifth wedding anniversary
was approaching and I thought it would be nice to write a little something to commemorate
our time together as husband and wife. I've also written a few poems about my two
children and the times we've had as they grew up. Now that I've finally started writing I
know I'll keep doing it as long as the inspiration is there and new ideas come along. As
my wife will attest, I express myself better with the pen than I do personally, so I better
keep writing.

## Yesterday

Where has the time gone?
Who is that stranger in the mirror?
Where is the young girl who used to be there?
And the young woman who took her place?
This is not the same face,
The pretty face that was admired and loved.
How did eighteen become eighty?
Where did the time go and leave me behind
When I am still eighteen in my mind?

Alice Jeffries
*New York, NY*


## Quiet

Oh quiet and peace I have dreamed
To hear nothing, what a delightful
Scheme.
After many years of noise and strife
I finally found my peace in life.
The mountains give me all I need,
The sounds I hear now comfort me.
To live in a city with noise and
Crime, is to live your life unhappy
Most of the time.
So every day I smile and say,
"Thank you, Lord, for a Quieter way."

Dennis Amato
*Middlebury Center, PA*

# Just Ask

Have a smile on your face for no reason.
Feel joy in your heart and it's out of season.
See a loved one make it through surgery.
Relieved from charges of perjury.
Surprising blessing with expectations of none.
Caught in stormy weather then out comes the sun.
Lonely in your soul then suddenly feel in love.
Drowning in an ocean then rescued from above.
Had a change of heart out of a world of hate.
Helped a needy stranger paid with pleasure so great.
Been led where to go when you lost your way.
Shown a lighted path in the deepest of the darken day.
These are all good rewards for our life to be.
But most times to blind of the true blessings to see.
Exception of a troubled life deception makes us fall.
Carrying blind anger to see no good at all.
Do you know to come to Jesus he is the guide of life.
Lifting all your burdens clearing your mind of strife.
Bow on your knees and ask Him to enter the door of your heart.
Once the Spirit's inside the blessings begin to start.
So tell all around you that on this day you're saved.
Be baptized with water leaving sin in the grave.
Born of the Spirit to allow God's love to shine through.
Love with all your heart, soul, and might is all He asks of you.

Kenneth Stephens
*Camy, KS*

# Untitled

I loved my mother when I was three
But God, He loved her more than me.
I didn't cry when she was gone
I was a big girl before too long.

Grandma came over every day
But them Grandma moved away.
I filled my bed with toys at night
And never slept without a light.

And when I married I loved so much
All he gave was not enough
He walked away and left me there
It was easy to say I didn't care.

And now my child runs to me
I hold him up so he can see
But he can't see the love inside
The love I just can't help but hide.

If he's strong he'll pull it free
If not, he'll grow up just like me
And the love I know he'll need so much
He may never find a way to touch.

But if I can teach him what I've lost
He may not have to pay the cost
God takes away, but He also gives
And maybe in me, a mother lives.

Jennifer Powell
*Moses Lake, WA*

# It Is the Good that Lies Within

When nations have turned red or blue
with common purpose hard to see.
Remember that a nation true
is just a sum of you and me!

It does not matter that the whole
may drift upon a common wave.
Seek that which lies within the soul
And take a step the world to save.

Love is often hard at the start
No guarantees that it will take.
Have faith in that within the heart
joy wilt be found no one can shake.

So see beyond the black and white
challenge untruths that may be given.
Instill trust and hope in all that's right,
it is the good that lies within.

For many the hope to survive
is met with selfishness and greed.
Please raise the bar for all to thrive,
someday it may be you in need!

Leesa A. McNeil
*Sioux City, IA*

## The Pain

The pain is just so deep
it's a gesture in my ever weep
I close my eyes to try to find
a place to call mine
then I think about the pain
and my eyes start to drain
the pain of losing
losing the ones I love
as they fly off like a dove
to go visit the man above

Tabbitha K. Steagall
*Silvis, IL*

## Sand

Cracks in the Sand,
We want you back again—
No Sea,
No Waves.
Because you're gone again.

You're the only one I see—
Not only the cracks
in the sand.
Now you've gone to the
Sea!

Shari A. Smirnes
*Warren, MI*

## Two Hearts

Early morning and I have returned from
the shorter version of my walk. It is the 29th of August
and I made it through the slow, hot, dog days of summer again.
The sun now holds a promise of afternoon heat,
it has not yet started to gather the dew from the
grass. I did as I forced my will and pant legs through
it. When a cloud interrupted the sun, I thought of…You.

There may be only one heart to a body. At times though,
two hearts can become one. Have mercy on both of…Them.

As the days grow shorter, the wild morning glories
stay longer. All that remains of the reaping is the
harvest. Thank you for letting me share your…Heart.

Where is my heart, you ask…Well.

It is drifting down a river, any river, pick one.
It is floating across an autumn sky, like
that skein of geese. It is wondering across the plains
with the wind. It is wading through timber to get to
a mountain top. It howls like a wolf. It sails
against a stiff breeze. It has endured capture and torture
been stole and broke and lonely. It is the only one I have,
I can't give it up…Anymore.

Mike Cooper
*Wever, IA*

# We Can't Put the Pieces Together Again

We laughed, we fought, and then we became friends
Sometimes the days flew by, sometimes they just wouldn't end.
So much of the time, almost always it seemed
We weren't living life, we were living out a bad dream.
We'd trade our sweat for dollars, our time for a chance
At the dream of a lifetime, but we never got to dance.
I play our song over and over, from beginning to end
But we can't put the pieces together again.

When the work day was done, we'd wash up and clock out
'Cause quitting time brought freedom, what life was about.
In the parking lot I'd wave goodbye, but I was never far behind
Followed you down the street of dreams, we'd eventually never find.
We talked about forever, new beginnings and passing trends
The time we had together, the love we shared as friends.
But if we unplug the clock, then time comes to an end
And we can't put the pieces together again.

We can't put the pieces together again
We can't control where we're going, we just accept where we've been
When one small part is missing, the message it sends
Is that we can't put the pieces together again…

Dan Gribovicz
*Harpersfield Township, OH*

# A Dream

I had a dream of being successful, taking it one day at time.
In my dream I wasn't scared, fear was far from my mind.
Dependent not on my own strength, but the strength of a Higher Power.
To see me through each day and every single hour.

In my dream I was confident and held my head high.
A pilot, flying a plane at great altitudes in the sky.
I saw clouds, which appeared to be angels with wings.
And a cloud that looked like it could've been the King of Kings.
I saw the heavenlies as beautiful as it could be.
At that moment, I knew that indeed I was free.
I was confident to know I was not alone.
Encompassed by angels and my Father, I knew I was not on my own.

There was a plane ahead guiding the way.
Assuring that I did not get lost or be led astray.
At times when I could not control the plane and it would steer away from
the path,
the plane ahead that guided the way would turn around ensuring I did not
crash.
It seems like every time I saw this plane I realized I was strong.
And I knew that the plane ahead was guiding me to whom I belonged.
I was protected by angels and held by the King.
Throughout the flight, I was covered by His precious wings.

And in the dream I flew with this one hope.
That God the Father would give me the strength to cope.

Shawnice Smith
*Decatur, GA*

286

# My Creed

I do not choose to be a Common, Man.
It is my right to be uncommon.
I seek opportunity=: = not security—
I do not wish to be a kept citizen,
I want to take the calculated risk—
to dream and to build, to fail and to succeed,
I refuse to barter incentive for a dole.
I prefer the challenge of life,
to guaranteed calm of Utopia.
Time is my only asset, God help me.
Use it wisely.
It is heritage to think and act for
myself.
Enjoy the benefits of my Creations,
and to face the world boldly and say,
"This I Have Done"

Allen H. Connors
*Augusta, GA*

# Handprints of Life

Jesus came into my life and I
Changed.
The way I was thinking
Changed.
My way of walking and talking
Changed.
With change
Came grace
Change
Came with Faith
Change
Came with Love
Change
Came with a new set of
Handprints for my life
Change.

Yvonne Middleton
*Hephzibah, GA*

## One Lucky Day

Darling, I love you
More than words can ever say
I've known joy beyond all expectations
Since you came into my life that lucky day.

For so very long I'd been lonely
Lonely in a way I could not define
I only knew deep within my heart
The love of my life I had yet to find.

I prayed to God that I would find him
This haunting stranger whose love was but a dream
For I could not shake the feeling
The feeling that true love was meant for me.

My prayers at last have been answered
You're all my dreams come true
Forever and a day, my love
My heart belongs to you.

Phyllis Dorn
*Victorville, CA*

This poem is dedicated to Don, my wonderful husband of thirty-four years. He has shown me that angels really do walk among us. I thank God every day for his love. I know that I am one girl who truly had "One Lucky Day" when he came into my life.

# The Unseen

My life has always been one of joy and despair
And through it all you were always there.
When I thought hope was too far out of reach,
You were always there to teach.
When darkness seemed endless like the night,
You were there to show me the light.
Without your guidance from above,
I never would have known true love.
The gifts you gave for me to keep
Will be my strength should I become weak.
My faith and devotion will be forever,
And our ties to each other will never be severed.
Thank you for never closing the door.
I could not ever love you more.

Amy Arena
*Jamesburg, NJ*

# Birds

Two nice small birds
Sitting on a tree
Another one joined them
Then there are three.
All cute birds have
Beaks that are sharp
Happily they spend time
Together they chirp.
All three birds make
Many different tricks
Two birds are very similar
As well as they're unique.
Two beautiful birds are
Very famous and tame
Also two birds have
Color that are same.
Two cute birds are
Well-known as crow
But the third bird has
Feather like a sparrow.

Faisal Hossain
*Piscataway, NJ*

I am a thirty-two year old man married with two children. Even with many hopes, all my dreams vanished due to a brain injury. While I was hoping for recovery, I tried to match words together. After trying I found that I can make good combination with words that sound the same. Then I tried to write poetry, when I was successful I wrote more. All of my poetry are for children and I spend a lot of time writing children's poetry. My wife Laila also encourages me to write and I look forward to writing more in the future.

## Each Advent Anew

Sweet Baby Jesus, we worship Thee
For what You are, for what you will be:
      our shinning light,
      comfort just right,
      hope in the night.

Child growing up in wisdom and stature,
teen so determined, courageous, and pure.
Man teaching others how to fully love
and grow spiritually, for life above.

Yet mostly you show us how to be true
to what God values our whole lives through:
How to stand firm, whate'er others may do.

Yes, Baby Jesus, each Advent anew
we study Your life and think about You,
thought not enough, 'cause our egos rush in
with worldly desires that lead us to sin
and hunger for pleasures that crowd our Your name
and make empty gestures in hope of mere fame.

Please, help us, dear Jesus, be true to You
as Christmas approaches and all yearlong, too.
Our precious Christ Baby, we need You, we do.
Thank You, dear Friend, Lamb of God, our Jesu.

Susanna-Judith Rae
*Avon, IN*

After reading details of the poetry contest, I prayed for God's will. On December 13, 2008, I realized I was indeed to write a poem. I closed my eyes, prayed, and soon saw a sweet little baby. Continuing to pray, I wondered if the baby was one of my adult sons or grandchildren as an infant. Suddenly, I understood that baby Jesus was to be the topic. After writing the first stanza, words I had heard in a recent dream popped into my mind: "growing in wisdom and stature." I added the words and continued to pray and write.

## Your Pay

I see you Eve when I go down the street
I look at each car to see if it is you I think
Of places where we have been I always look
But you are not there when will the hurt end
When will I find you there?
I remember the day I stopped by your place
I knocked on the door I don't think you heard me
The first time you might have been vacuuming
We talked for a while you were sweet as you always are
I had not seen you for a couple of months But
I missed you a lot we talked for a while more
Then you said you have to take a shower and off you
went a few moments later you called me
We made love that day I miss you a lot
God I was wrong when I left you and I regret
it each day life is not bad now but I think
of you a lot and How I miss you Remember the
Day we drove to Ohio and you were so happy
Because that day was for you.

George Jenkins
*Pittsburg, PA*

# Golden Sunrise

Children without faith
The wings of an angel, the horns of the devil
The innocence that was easily forgotten
His murderous eyes, her killer smile
Everything dies the pain is mild
A golden sunset in the form of a child
You speak his name without distaste
A loving look for a lovely face
A love for those you held dear
No more memories that bring back fear
You hear her laugh, you shed a tear
You think these memories are quite queer
With no sins of your own
A good life of your own
A good life, a clean soul; a spirit no one can control
The fair existence; The happy ending
you reunite, a dream never-ending

Daniel Miller
*Mastic, NY*

# If I Could . . .

If I could learn to soar like an eagle,
surpassing fears that always held me back,
I'd validate my right to being here
and imprint my footsteps in the sand.

If I could face those who destroyed my chances
and made my life impossible to live,
I'd understand they are the ones in darkness
and have no longer any power over me.

If I could rise above my daily sorrows
and see myself for what I'm really worth,
it'll dawn on me I still have my tomorrows
and what I make of them is really up to me.

If I could stop looking over my shoulder
and choose to leave behind my heavy load,
perhaps I'd find the joyous sound of laughter
and even reach and touch the face of God.

Myrna I. Figueroa-Colon
*Rio Piedras, PR*

# The Thanksgiving Archer

Family familiar, gathered together:
Some casual words—perhaps
aimed in jest—
Struck their target and secretly smarted.

Seasons slip past:
One wonders now—does he
Brazenly breeze through life—
exuberant and unaware
That his spoken arrows still sting?

Edith Phillips
*Old Greenwich, CT*

Holding family get-togethers ... We all attend them with the hope of experiencing warm fuzzy feelings, but family dynamics can be unpredictable. After such occurrence, putting pen to paper was therapeutic for me.

# Stem the Flow

Oh God forgive this chore of mine
That I must undertake.
It is a job that must be done,
Although my heart will break.
This Greyhound dog's life that I must end
Raced with all its heart and now must go!
To make room for a thousand more
(God can't we stem the flow?)
It is the breeders that do not care
How many pups they spawn.
Through greed they hand the mess to me,
My head it rests upon.
They want the public to have and see
This miracle called birth,
To race the dogs a few months or so,
Then find they've lost their worth.
So send these breeders and the public to spend the day
With me amid the oven's breath;
And I will show them how this dutiful dog's life ends
Through no miracle called "death!"

Beverly Page
*Topsfield, MA*

## Life's Journey

Life is a journey we live it every day.
Life is a journey we make plans along the way.
Life's journey sometimes goes another way.
Life's journey it could be for the good or not
So good, but we go on the journey anyway.
Life's journey can make us happy or sad.

Life is a journey and alive we are and glad.
Life's journey we sometimes go on it alone.
Life's journey we are never alone with God.
Life's journey live it and be grateful.

Rita Whitley
*Southfield, MI*

Education: Rockhurst University Continuing Education Center, Certificate Program developing Successful Training Programs for the Workplace 2006. Wayne State University, Certificate Program Train-the-Trainer 2005, Advanced Train-the-Trainer training 2007 Spring Arbor Universtiy, Bachelor of Arts Degree, Major: Management of Human Resources 1991-1992 Wayne County Community College, Associate of Arts Degree, Major: Management Minor: Marketing 1971-1980

## This Tear

It starts with an emotion that sets the mood
The mood forms a twinkle in the eye
Like a star in the clear sky
The twinkle shines with great intensity
Thus, a drop of water appears
This drop is full of sadness, happiness, and love
That shower my heart from above
Our eyes meet knowing what lies ahead
Feelings of passion form and mend
A continuous link that will not end
Saltwater that nourishes our souls
This tear I longed to see
I would like to be
Once touched by my flesh
It sheds any doubt
Of how things will turn out
'Cause this tear
This tear is preserved
'Til eternity

Glenn Ward
*Sioux Falls, SD*

## To a Statue of Jeanne D'Arc on a Much Traveled Road

Look down you saintly Maid and see me here
Beneath your horse's hooves who stands and loves,
Or do you think of France, so far yet near,
Unconscious of the wind and rain and doves
Which build their nests 'tween scabbard and hard thigh.
O ride your steed, raise high your tarnished steel.
Look up to God see not who pass you by.
Mind not their slights, their insults do not feel.
You, who so many victories have known,
This one you cannot win for all your pain,
Be not distressed, you are yourself of stone.
Perhaps men think 'tis they that you disdain.
Look you not down for you can see me not.
Dream on, O Maiden fair, of things forgot.

Thomas W. DeJohn
*Havertown, PA*

## Reality

Captured my heart,
          my soul,
               my mind
    From reaction of your action, it all does exist.
The Aleutians, the Rockies, Appalachin, and Himilayas
Formed over time
          mere reactions
               imagine that.
   The clock is ticking,
          so the cycle continues.
   The Earth was one body—of say what?
          ICE
     The reaction of your actions.
Seven continents, five oceans that feed all the rivers and seas,
          rain forest, even deserts.
     Gave it all to us,
          what do we do?
     Contaminate, destroy, eliminate your gifts.
Whoever said that the very air we breathe is a damn guarantee.
    After all we have virtually destroyed the ozone layer
          How smart can this be?
My heart,
       my soul,
          my mind
             you have captured
                yet I have done you wrong.
What to expect and what I may dream are two different things
          For what I know
The actions are great,
          Your reactions even greater.

Cassandra I. Coleman
*Avondale, AZ*

301

# The Future

If we but knew what lay at hand
If we could gaze into the morrow
If we could see what God hath planned
If we could know each joy and sorrow

If we could see the future unwrap
If tomorrow could become today
If we could read our life like a map
If we knew what things lay at bay

But as I mull this wish in my mind
My desire is losing its flavor
For God perhaps is being kind
And not letting us know is a favor

For we must live as the Lord hath planned it
And maybe that's part of the fun
In letting the future remain a secret
And taking what may as it comes

Joan Turetsky
*Briarwood, NY*

## My Pen

I've had many of conversations,
about my pen and the terrible condition,
that I keep it in.
Now when I write with my pen,
it doesn't seem to work like it did then.
Pilot V5, extra fine,
If it was ever found,
they'd know it was mine
because everyone knows about my pen,
and the terrible condition I keep it in.
My pen is there to help me out.
It seems to care when I'm in doubt.
Even when there's nothing to write
I get my pen
and hold it tight.
All of the sudden, it begins to spin.
I turn to look and realize then,
the terrible condition that my pen is in.
My pen
seems to be
my only friend!

Michelle E. Shyne
*Riverside, CA*

I am the mother of a teenage daughter. We reside in Southern California. The poem "My Pen" was inspired by a friend who kept her pens in terrible condition and I would complain to her every time I saw her. On the other hand, I kept my writing utensils in perfect condition. I like to collect pens. I believe they are pretty. I enjoy the different colors and the way a pen expresses my mood. I have a writing set with my name inscribed on it and I dare anyone to touch it.

# To Dance with Time

The music life plays begins like a romantic symphony.
We waltz about and glide through life's mystical coalition
Gripping youth's every breath,
Inhaling the years as they pass us by in hopes
of living one more day.
And to our surprise, once fatigue disappears,
We admire the cool and summer days,
full moon nights and brisk changes in seasons.
In appreciation of this miraculous beauty that surrounds
our existence,
We exhale from the joys of hearing a baby's first cry;
Remembering seniors that have passed us by
as time makes room for the recycling of life.
Hence, our invitation to living is a dance with time.

Thelma Berry-Williams
*Columbia, MD*

# The Sweet Singing Angel

Could I ask a question
What could be soothing
And bring such warm comfort
Early in the morning that must take its course
When a truly beautiful measure must occur
And time itself is suspended
As only the sweet words from an angel
Can shield us from the world
When strife and agony is absent and forgotten
And it is this angel that stands shining before us
Harmony is once again restored
And the grace she gives each of us
Are the wings that make us soar higher
Than we could ever hope to have done
Her precious voice lifts our hearts to overcome our anguish
And brings us closer to the wondrous stars
Where these shadows that imprison and cloud our weary eyes
No longer exist when the song of the angel sets us all free
Brightening our days
And giving us such a serenity
So that we can sleep
And dream once more
And wake to a new day
In which we shed no more tears

Justin Sarracino
*Florence, KY*

# The Braggart

I can fly a great big kite
And I fly an Ultralite.
Yes, I fly an aeroplane
And I tap dance in the rain.
I can sail into a port
And I play most any sport.
With my old blue sneakers on,
Walked the New York Marathon.
Music? Never paid the rents
(I play seven instruments).
Education was a breeze
(I have three post-grad degrees).
When they yearned to hear my views,
I was on "Eyewitness News."
If asked, "What is new, sir?"
I'll say, "TV producer."
"Expert Witness," they called me;
Killed the Bill and kept them free!
Of all the things within my reach,
Best of all is when I teach.
Thinking what else you can do?
Firstly, "to your heart be true."
What is new within my sight?
Chuck it all—if I could write.

Arthur Stein
*Tafton, PA*

## Arterial Damage

The heart really does break
As love slips bleeding
Into rank puddles
On the back street:
Arterial damage.

Brilliant sparks upsurged,
Licked the sun,
Burnt out,
Cooled.
Ashes
Float on pools
Of red.

Like the sun lost its way
In some Manhattan alleyway;
Caught midst phallic spires,
It lay there,
Bleeding light.

While heart pumped
Love, in vain,
Spurting crimson,
Breaking in the dark:
Arterial damage.

Rosemary Rizzotto
*Reseda, CA*

As love illuminates us, so the loss of love casts us into darkness. This poem is about that darkness felt with the loss of a lover. The heart breaks in many ways, but I feel is universally felt as a loss of light. I wished to convey this contrast in my poem. I am a visual artist, as well as a poet. The arts and my faith are the methods I utilize when life turns dark, when the sun is taken away.

# Afloat Again

I was a ship that you kept dry-docked
My tongue tied in a sailor's knot
My emotions wrapped tight like a sail
Waiting to be unfurled
My prose help prisoner
Battened down below your hatches
A slave being held in your squalor
In your neglect
In your greed
I push my nose toward the porthole
I breathe in a creative breath
I see but do not feel the cresting wave

I am that ship at sea now
My hull is caressed by the gentle slapping of your calm tides
I have always loved you
Like the winds that fill my sails
Your currents direct me
Leading me
My verse is my compass
My prose strong as an anchor's chain
I feel sometimes I trespass
But for all who put pen to paper
I claim this as my own domain

Felipe Rosa
*Bridgeport, CT*

## Inside Out

It's hard to regret and have no pain
But you are the only one to accept the change

Wrapped like a mummy with no navigation
You can only blame yourself and not your situation

Re'A'ppear in the faces of your shadow not traces
Reaping what you sew in all the wrong places

Make no mistakes because they have been made
Go right on ahead you cannot be afraid

For time has gone and now is the time
Do for yourself and commit no crime

No child left behind so don't be a fool
Go seek your talents push all the way through

No one noticed nothing not needed nor known
Complete control contains constant conflicts
Sustain some smarts supply simple services
Dedication drives distance direction doing deeds
Better believe best before beauty
Losers looks lostfully last left lonely

So choose a path before it's already chosen
Keep high almighty for he has already risen
So walk tall until actions are spoken
Keep all in mind take time to stop look and listen

DeBrien L. Howard
*Dallas, TX*

# 13 Favorite Things

I can bet that you can't yet guess
The things that I will not let you forget.
Now let's start with something fun,
does anyone like to play in the sun?
Are you like me, someone who likes
Hannah Montana or Camp Rock on TV?
How about Rock 'n' Roll, Pop, or Funk?
How about that author, Cornelia Funke?
And I also like magazines.
Just to tell you I adore the color green.
My favorite holiday is Earth Day, I also
love my birthday!
I really like to draw and write.
My dad and I also like to ride our bikes.
Now all I want to know is . . .
What do you like?

Skylur Clay
*E. Wenatchee, WA*

# I Never Let Go

As I look out into the dark, starry night I feel you in my heart.

I'll never let go of the strong love I have for you, never letting go of how your smile enriches my life for when I fall asleep I see you in my dreams.

Holding you in my arms, kissing your soft lips, embracing your body as I know that my love for you will last forever.

"I never let go!" would be our force that will bind us together even closer as time passes by.

The beauty that surrounds you as I look into your eyes, Oh! I yearn to touch your soul once more with the flame of desire.

The roaring fire of passion that cries out to the world from both of us that nothing nor no one could cool off this rage of passion.

For you open the door to my heart which once was closed. Now my heart is filled with joy.

I'll never let go of my love for you nor will I denounce any feelings of how the very thought of you brings everything in my life into focus.

I love you now and forevermore. I never let go!

Wendell P. Versher
*Phoenix, AZ*

I'm the fifth child of fifteen brother and sisters. I was born September 21, 1955. I grew up loving the Cubs and booing the Chicago White Sox, yes, I am from a small suburb of Robbins, Illinois. I wanted to play pro baseball, I love to play drums, sing, fish, and I love to write. I was inspired to write this poem about a beautiful woman who holds a special place in my heart. Words of beautiful should rain upon her like rain drops from heaven, I love her with all my heart.

# What is Black?

Black is Death
The depth of fright
The scream
That fills the darkened night
A successful kill
The signature on someone's will

Black is Silence
The fur of a cat
The demon-like wings
Of a fluttering bat
The dripping blood on vampire fangs
The empty house with its thunderous bangs

Black is Sorrow
The ink in a writer's quill
The words
That give you a sudden chill
The breath of decaying prey
The funeral in your grave you lay

Black is Gone
The stars where the ravens fly
The long,
Deep, depressing sigh
The bed where you moan and cry
The happiness as it will age and die

Christine Jurek
*Casper, WY*

## History Speaks

In a place that reaches out to you with ancient voices.
A place that when you breathe in you breathe history.
Where the soil you step on has drunk in the blood of heroes.
A place where the mountains tell tales of glory.
This is Sparta.

In a time where God's laughed at men's struggles.
When sword and shield were the judge, jury and executioner.
When men still held glory above all else.
A time of kings, heroes, warlords, and legends.
This is Sparta.

In a life where you had to fight to live.
A life where pride and honor were more important than anything.
Where your only goal in existing was so your name would be
remembered.
A life where your memory could carry on over the centuries.
This is Sparta.

A life few can imagine and hundreds long for.
A time of myth and legend we can only dream about.
A place we long to just belong to.
A memory, a story, a song, a picture, a movie, that will live forever.
This is Sparta.

Bobbie Jo Guitreau
*Geismar, LA*

# Life

When you feel like the world has given up on you
You feel trapped in your own skin
You feel naked, unclean, unwanted, and lost within yourself
You feel scared, lonely, and forgotten
You feel abandoned but the world you thought you knew
You feel tears about to drip slowly down your face
You feel weak, depressed and angry
You feel this torment tearing you up inside
You feel like your life is doomed forever
You feel like nothing but an empty shell
that has been kicked around a lot
You feel like your heart has nothing else to give but an empty path
That has no past, present, or future for you
When there is only misery that takes you on the same ride
Which means life is nothing more than illusion we all see
While we set up ourselves for disappointment and lies
We hurt, we cry, we bleed, but there is nobody out there that cares
enough to help
There is so much pain that grows inside yourself
That you don't know where to put it
You feel like death is the only way out
You feel the touch of a gun in your hand
You feel the warmth of happiness starting to appear
A smile, that will take you home to where you feel you belong
You imagine a world beautiful and free
Where you feel safe, loved, and wanted
Angels that sing and fly all around you
Telling you there are people who love you
So stay, you are not ready to fly always
Please stay, please stay, please stay

Maria Rodriguez
*Schenectady, NY*

## The Letter

Today, as I opened the letter, my heart skipped a beat.
It was from my only grandson, the writing was not so neat.
I'm writing you today, he says, there may not be a tomorrow.
The battle zone is raging, I've never seen such horror.
I think of you often, dear Grandmama, the letter went on to say,
Like when I was a little boy and would run out to play.
I can still hear you saying, "You are my pride and joy!"
Oh, wouldn't it be Heaven to be again, just a little boy.
So Grandmama, I still love you . . . but the enemy is drawing near,
So I'll just close this letter.
Oh, my heart is filled with such fear.
The morning was oh so cloudy . . . the thunder it did roar.
As I sat in my chair by the window, I heard a loud knock at the door.
There a soldier was waiting, his eyes held no clue.
He looked so sad as he started, "I regret to inform you . . ."
My heart seemed to struggle . . . his words lost in the thickening air.
As I lifted my eyes to Heaven . . . "Oh, God, hear my prayer."
Please let this war be over, no one will ever win,
No one else needs to hear, "You are the next of kin."
I think of all the boys who are fighting to make the world stay free,
Throw down your guns and come home . . .
Do it for my grandson and me.

Clara R. Deas
*Rock Hill, SC*

# All the Good Things to Come

You finish your stew and pick up a brew
and stare at the old Panasonic.
You burp, you grin, you wipe off your chin
as you drift to a state catatonic.

The knock on the door brings your eyes off the floor,
it's your friends with laughs and a toke.
So you taste of the lotus and then fail to notice
your ambition depart with the smoke.

While you're comfortably sat you grow steadily fat,
pointing fingers at everything dumb.
Nothing falls in your lap so you wait like a sap
for all of the good things to come.

Jack Davidson
*Sparks, NV*

## Yesteryear

I would like to take a stroll down memory lane,
Back to the time when life was so carefree, quiet and plain.

I was young, and tomorrow was so far away,
No need to worry about the future, that would be another day.

Years passed, and tomorrow did come for me,
I married my true love, which I thought would be for eternity.

He gave me a red rose the day we were wed,
Attached with a beautiful ribbon was a card that said,

"With all my love forever, and may all your dreams come true,
I promise that I will always be there for you."

When you're with someone you love, the world seems
cheerful and bright,
But sometimes things happen along the way and you see life in a
different light.

Time changes everything and eventually we drifted apart.
He left me all alone, and with a broken heart.

Oh, how I wish I could go back and take another stroll
down memory lane,
Relive the days of yesteryear, when life was so quiet and plain.

I know that I can't go back, and that I must live each day as though it
were my last,
Think only good of the future and forget the past.

Keitha I. Allen
*Mansfield, OH*

# Bailey My Bichon

Twenty-two pounds of white fluffy fur frolicking in the yard
If you are passing by you don't have to be on guard.
He would never attack you but might lick too much
You look into those sparkling dark eyes, you want to touch.

Friends were visiting one night, we served Baileys Irish Cream
Some was spilled accidentally, the dog thought he was in a dream.
He was licking it up as fast as he could
Thus the name Bailey seemed to fit him real good.

He loves to go for a ride and look out the window of the car
It makes him feel really special and he hopes you go far
Go get a lotto ticket, go to the Dairy Queen or go to the park
He sits there like a mighty king, you won't ever hear him bark.

Ancestors of Bichons were circus entertainers and loved to please
To impress you Bailey jumps, spins around and drops to his knees.

My leg was hurting, Bailey was close by, he didn't want to see me cry
He would lay his head on my leg, hoping my eyes would stay dry.

Speak to him, he cocks his head as if he knew exactly when you said
Sometimes I think Phi Beta Kappa has messed with his head.

My life is exciting and fun since the day Bailey was found
I love him so much, I hope I never have to hear his last sound.

Georganna Morrison
*Sarasota, FL*

I am a mother of four and grandmother of eight and counting with two twin boys due soon. My husband Richard and I are blessed with these wonderful children plus Bailey our Bichon who adds an additional sparkle to our lives. After a kidney transplant and turning seventy a few years ago, I really couldn't play tennis anymore and I wasn't hitting the golf ball as far as I used to, so I decided I needed a new hobby. Without a clue as to what I was doing, I decided to write poetry for my family and friends.

# This Is Today

Yes, this is Today, this is the only time in our lives
we will have this day.
For every day is new and different.

Not many hours ago it was tomorrow.

And soon it will be yesterday.

Live it as though it will be the last day you will have for the rest of your
life.  Enjoy every minute of this God-given day.  Reach out to others and
make someone smile today.

For today will soon be gone.

Weave every minute into hours
with Love, Happiness, Patience, and Faith.

For today will soon be gone.

Think not of yesterday's problems or worries of tomorrow.
Live Today and make it a loving masterpiece given to us from
God above.

For Today will soon be gone.

Helen Dalleske
*Rescue, CA*

## Sad

Cold as ice
Frosty bitter
Frozen cry
One breath
Left to spare
Finely the last breath is gone

McKenna S. McNamara
*Phoenix, AZ*

## Business Week

Business is busy people are rushing
got to get to the part from here to there
phones are ringing, people are talking
company owners are marketing
and working very hard to get deadlines
concentrate and meetings to end
time is moving the days are about to end
employees are tired looking
is tomorrow eight to five is our shift
making the world move around is our job
for the next day we are happy
clocking out
see you tomorrow and have a nice day

Debbie L. Hill
*Kinston, NC*

# I Think I Love You

I think I love you
I can't be sure
The only problem is I can't tell you

I think of you every day
My mind is full
I know I need you in every way

Just one touch I got from you
Buterflies all askew
Now without you I am blue

I see you every night in my dreams
Holding me, loving me
When I awake I want to scream

I don't know what the future holds
For you and I
Right now inside I feel so cold

They think it's love
I can't be sure
You're my happiness sent from above

I don't know what I'm going to do
But in my heart
I think I love you.

Jamie L. Wilson
*Tomah, WI*

This poem is about wondering if I am in love or not. I thought I knew what love was and now I know I was wrong. Now I am a mother of two beautiful girls and I am truly in love with my boyfriend of five years. Love doesn't always come when you want it to but when it does, hold on to it and never let it go.

## Romeo

Strong, sensual, articulate, intriguing, loyal,
A thriving Nubian king.
Sweet, intelligent, an African god.
Truthful, honest, poetic, my first real lover.
Though I've never felt his breath hit my lips
Or his pulse near my heart,
I love the mere mention of "Romeo."
Built for this world by a strong-minded spirit and a divine soul.

Blessed by faith and wisdom to withstand the
Tremendous love anyone has to give.
Seen by many, felt only by me.
His eyes spray my soul like a sweet drop of honeydew on a warm Indian
summer.
He's the drop of cream in my 4:30 a.m. coffee.
He's the rippling of a million moons.
He's the faithfulness of a new love.

He's the willingness in my heart when I want to let go.
Joy is what I feel when my tears intertwine with his soul.
I am amazed how love has granted my fondest wish,
To be made love to by a true and loyal man.
He's the momentous occasion that I celebrate daily.
He's "Romeo."

Kendra Minniefield
*Selma, AL*

## Yellow Suicide

Yellow oranges!
Yellow oranges, you too!

Childish giggles and sweet kisses
The taste of oranges on your tongue, the smell of you tangled
in my sheets and on my pillow.
The imprint of the way you once laid stays.

"It's over!"
"You're breaking my heart!"

Sobbing and crying;
Pain going through my body;
A sword piercing my chest,
Stomping on my heart with your cold stance and your cold stare,
No common sense is coming through.

Sharp blades on the counter.

Suicide.

Let the blade drag across and vertically down,
Spills on the floor like orange juice,
The last thing I see before I succumb:
Yellow oranges split in two,
Just like me and you.

Azaria Gamble
*Martinsville, VA*

# This Is Me

I am a daughter and a sister
I am a mother and a woman
I am mostly quiet and I am shy
I am hurt but I am whole
I have a heart as pure as gold
I am lonely as well as surrounded
I am afraid but I take chances
I am lost but I was found
I am giving although others have taken
I am strong but I feel so weak
I am sick and I'm tired
But I am healthy and I am awake
I am dazed and confused
But I know what I want
I am soft-spoken on the outside
But inside I feel as if I'm screaming
But no one is around to hear
I am mad at myself for the choices I've made
But this is my life
I should have no shame
I am a daughter and a sister
I am a mother and a woman
This is my story
This is my life
But overall, this is me

Marie Sickler
*Saugerties, NY*

# Reflexing Back

Remember Sodom and Gomorrah
The city that was destroyed and burned
Has it returned
From a nation built on God's word
That no longer serves the living meaning
But feeds off the inner feelings
Of selfishness
Poisoning the true meaning of Freedom
Forcing a nation into believing
Against
The knowledge of what it was taught
Destroying the moral values that were so strongly sought
Now has become so easily bought
With no care of the cost
As lives are lost over a foreign oil pipeline
The remembrance of Ground Zero soon forgotten over time
As we face more job losses and houses' for sale signs
It's time we draw the line
And quit replacing God with laws
Life for death
Truth for lies
And begin changing fear
Into courage
That will seek the solution based on the facts

Michael A. Bass
*Katy, TX*

## Mom I Love You

I did not see my mother's nakedness
while I was in her womb.
Who gave me the privilege
when I was growing up?
Who gave me the privilege
when I was in her room?
Mom, I love you.
Mom, I love you more.
But for nine months I was in your womb.

Paul N. de Mauriac
*Centerbrook, CT*

## Peace, Love, and Inspiration

I want to write a life villanelle
A sonnet for my heart
A haiku life beat
But like winter's pallor
Within the cold Nevada Mountain snows
Inspiration is covered by emotion
So when will I bloom again
When I am sixty
When I am seventy
As life and dust settle
Peace and love in my time
As inspiration's soul thaws through

Denise Ferguson
*Reno, NV*

326

# Why I Wait

You hold me down when times get rough,
and hold me up when life gets tough.
You offer a shoulder for me to cry on
and a friendship I can always rely on.

You guide my soul through the roughest of seas,
and lend me your hand when I fall to my knees.
You give me strength and you show me the way
and make me believe it really will be okay.

You know just how to melt this cold heart of ice
and offer me wonderful words of advice.
You shine some light on things I never saw
and see beauty in the most hideous flaws.

You have more faith in me than the rest,
and that's why I'll always push you to do your best.
This is why waiting for one another
is so worth my while.

Nicole Lewandowski
*Norristown, PA*

## In the End

My friend please remember in the end,
As I've been told there will be streets of gold.
So never fear when the end is near and you, my friend,
May walk the streets of gold.
Let the heavens open up my friend, remember what I've been told,
And when the end is near we can walk those streets of gold.
So, don't fear and grab that cloud my friend
And ride it and this is what I've been told
About streets of gold.

Ricky L. Sisk
*Madisonville, KY*

## Clouds

What makes the clouds
    hang in the sky
No one knows
    the reason why
In different sizes
    and assorted colors
Why are they hanging up
    there so high
Like a highway
    in the sky
There has to be a reason
It's for the different season

Geneva McCrayer
*Dallas, TX*

## Devoured by Darkness, a Victim of Despair . . .

Sweet solitude stolen
       by a soldier of misfortune.
Sinking, sinking . . .
       devoured by darkness.
Save me!
       What is this beast that wipes away my smile?
       That which robs me of my power and worth,
       crippling my thoughts, my imagination,
       me?

It has taken away my initiative,
       reaping happiness, locking it away for none to see.
Defeat and despair
       hamper the ability to exist in here . . .
       a mere shell, enveloped in dismay.
Lost and alone
       the answers are buried in unearthed stone.
The deep wrinkles of the mind
       drawing me inward
       deeper, deeper . . . until I am no more.

Michelle L. Henkels
*Bloomington, MN*

## I Love You, Katrina

A demented mind fosters the key to sanity.
Last night as I was woken from my world of sleep,
I awoke to discover my dreams were not those of sweet fantasy,
but of bitter reality.
And as I touched the cold where your warmth once was,
Tears began to sting my eyes.
I heard the breeze echo with the last words you said to me, I love you.
In remembering those words passing your soft, beautiful lips,
The quietness of silence pushes me and my imagination,
Brings you here to this place, where on so many nights,
You peacefully slept right next to your man, Naiem.
I smile to myself behind a stream of tears
And I reach out to touch your beautiful, gorgeous lips.
This attempted touch, the image of you returning
to the realm of my mind.
Now, with even visions of you seemingly gone,
My heartbreak pushes me into an embrace with reality.
I discover you are more than just this man's heart.
You are the rhythm of my heartbeat.
Therefore, I'll never be able to stop loving you, Katrina.

Naiem Firouzmandi
*Toledo, OH*

## Beautiful Smile, Shine in this World

Beautiful smile, how wonderful you are
How you light up my world when my
Darkest days seem so gray
Beautiful smile touching my soul
Guide me with happiness that's not far to reach
Hold me, captivate me with a kiss of your kindness
Joy of the heart smiling from within
Beautiful smile never leave my side
Remind the world that it is a better day ahead
A brighter future that's not dead
A rainbow to see at the end of mankind's destiny
This beautiful smile I have to share
Smile on the problems of others
Smile on the innocent being robbed of their happiness
Beautiful smile shine on the poverty that has stricken our world today
Breathe that beautiful smile I love so much
Help me to see there is more to live than the sadness we see

Amy Long
*Chattanooga, TN*

# The Depression

I'm depressed, stressed,
And my problems don't cease, but recycle and refresh.
No longer in school but I'm still taking a test.
I wish for hurt they made a bulletproof vest.
More than less, they set free criminals
And the innocent they arrest.
There's no jobs to work, shorten schedule hours.
Electricity low, no energy for power,
The planes crashed the two towers,
And we got sewage leaks, so everyone taking dirty showers . . . or bath.
Our kids following the wrong path
They can cut up dimes but can't divide an equation in math . . .
Or perhaps, they, too, city bound so they don't study maps.
Little girls too busy sitting on every Santa's lap.
No audience but their bodies clap.
No wings to flap, so we can't fly away
To another destination
So somebody can understand or show appreciation.
Our pockets deflate while prices are in inflation.
Everybody talking but no communication.
Everyone just wasting time
'Cause as long as there's depression,
We will continue scuffing dimes.

Opal C. Collins
*Jonesboro, GA*

# A Prison Feeling

Being locked down is a hard situation.
You can feel depressed, discouraged, and devastation.
There is always a reason to keep holding on.
It's usually a family member or someone from back home.
You can do your time, or let your time do you.
Everyone should make the most of it, there are things to do.
Whether you better yourself socially or education-wise,
make yourself a person that stops stealing or telling lies.
Yes, there is that humbleness that you have to find within yourself.
You come in broke and alone, and can leave full of love and wealth.
When you have all the time to think and plan, one can leave with their
dreams and goals in hand.
There are times when dealing with people can cost you.
With some patience and the Lord, it won't exhaust you.
Many people get letters, visitation, and have phone calls,
But just as many, or more, have nobody at all.
If the world could only relate to the feelings inside,
I guarantee even the ignorant ones couldn't leave those people high and
dry.
It's true what they say about doing a crime and time,
yet it's unbelievable how many innocent people have crossed the prison
lines.
There's so many worthy people within the walls of the "forgotten cities."
What an impact it would have if the community could show some pity.

Michelle L. Sedeno
*Sunrise, FL*

# My Africa

Africa my motherland
my land of the kings and the animals
my beautiful culture and the tribes
my field of my idea and my dream.

Africa my Diaspora
I have prayed to find your help
I have sung for the world to hear you
I have cried to all the kings of the world.

Africa my sound of the heaven
the source of the intellectual powers
the door of the prayers and the singers
I want to see you again and protect you.

Africa my wishes of the all
the top of the circle
the star of the tongues
I want to see you again and protect.

the hundreds of people dead every second
the tears of the innocents spray the trees
the birds of the sky dance on the deaths
the volunteers bring the wind
I want to be with you.

The plants always need the water
the Africans need the peace
the killers must stop to kill
the hope and the peace need to be the all
I want to be with you.

Jean D. Ngoyi
*Raleigh, NC*

334

## Shanghai of Yore

A very vivid recollection of Shanghai occurred when the family attended
a theater one evening.
Academy Award winning movie "Wings" was premiering with Buddy
Rodgers, Clara Bow, and Richard Arlen starring.
It had been raining most of the day
As streets glistened from lights reflected our way.

We stood in a line huddled under umbrellas
as a chilling wind swept through.
The line stretched around the block
and something else was stretching too.
We gazed down in abject disbelief.
As a number of coolies and beggars were laying in the street's gutters
with considerable grief.

They were hunched with their backs pressed to the curb.
Covered with wet newspapers trying to sleep in their suburb.
Their bodies lined the curb for two long blocks.
We began to comprehend the true meaning of poverty, misery and
degradation.
Doesn't this define hard knocks?

Antonio Perez
*Los Alamitos, CA*

## Man on the Street

Help him.
Save him please.
He's a man walking the street.
He has no place to sleep
and nothing to eat.
Help him, save him, please.

Tell him the old, old story
about Jesus and His glory.
Show him the way to go,
God's glory to know.

Reach out your hand,
There is much need in this land.
Reach out to the man
on the street.

Patricia Newville
*Stockton, KS*

Contrary to public opinion, not all homeless people are alcoholics or drug addicts. Most homeless people don't even want to live that way, but the system can't or won't help them. I know, I've been homeless most of my life. Even with a roof over my head, I still feel homeless because people misunderstand me and really have no desire to know me. This poem is titled "Man on the Street." You could easily replace man with woman or child.

# Ever Greet

Gliding into port
On water so flat,
Our last remembered storm
That would sicken a rat.

Tall buildings and colors
Are seen in the sky,
With white puffin clouds
And a warm summer high.

With our deck full of cargo
Moving all ahead slow,
Our ship for all seasons
In the water, rides low.

We slide into port now
The cranes coming near,
There's lifting and yelling
Watch the cargo disappear.

The ship is now empty
As the crew heads for shore,
For drinking and dancing
And quite a bit more.

William Olesky
*Kearny, NJ*

# Take the Time

Take the time to say I love you to those you do.
Take the time to listen, it will be a blessing to you.
Take the time to pray, it will guide your pathway.

Take the time to say, "I'm sorry" when you need to.
Take the time to enjoy nature, it will truly amaze you.
Take the time to learn new things, this can be a life-long quest.
Take the time to nurture friendships, they will warm your heart.

Take the time to make new friends, you can never have too many.
Take the time to read, it will open up your mind.
Take the time to meditate, it will relax the body.
Take the time to workout, it will help in many ways.

Take the time to pursue a hobby, it may end up a career.
Take the time to travel, exploring our beautiful world.
Take the time to connect with family, they will love you always.
Take the time to help the needy, God will bless you for it.

Take the time to enjoy the simple pleasures in life, since the best things
in life are free.
Take the time to improve yourself, you will love the result.
Take the time to enjoy life by slowing down.
Take the time to find the good in everyone and let that be your focus.
Remember to take time while you still have time to take.

Stephen Balbach
*Saginaw, MI*

I am married with two grown children, Sara and Erich. Sara, the youngest, was the
first to marry. I composed this poem for her wedding. On July of 2005 at her wedding
reception, I read this poem. My inspiration for the poem came to me as I was thinking
about Sarah and how fast she grew up. As I was thinking about her and other events in
my life I realized how important it is to slow down and take the time to do things that will
enrich your life and the others around you. I used this special occasion to share some
fatherly advice with my daughter while I had her complete attention. I hope anyone who
reads this poem will "take the time" to enrich their life as well.

## Rodeo Time

This old cowboy is old and gray.
He sits in his rocking chair and rocks all day.
But in his mind he's far away,
Yes, in his mind he's in Rodeo Time.

He sees himself young and bold.
He thinks of all the horses he's rode.
He sees the arenas and all the bright lights,
All the bulls he had to fight.
Yes, he just sits and rocks all day,
But in his mind he's far away.
He's in younger days.

When he tries real hard he can hear the cheers,
He smells those horses, he can hear the steers.
People look as they go by,
All they see is a crazy old cowboy waiting to die.

What they don't know, that behind that grin,
The crazy old cowboy is riding again.

Betty Ragsdell
*Paragould, AR*

# Angels Whisper

Angels whisper: Come on now you can do it, go to the light and let your
life begin to unfold.
Angels whisper: Keep trying, words will get better with time, I'm told.
Angels whisper: Go, go peddle like the wind, oops, it's okay. You have
time to do what you showed.
Angels whisper: A confusing time for you. You have ups and downs and
seems you carry a big load.
Angels whisper: It's your special day. Remember this day, a day to have
and to hold.
Angels whisper: Now you have little ones, you think, came from your
own mold.
Angels whisper: Years have come and gone, and you feel you're still
paying on bills you've once owed.
Angels whisper: Gained a lot over the years and put in memory the
things you've sold.
Angels whisper: You're not the youth you used to be and things are hard
and slow, since you've grown old.
Angels whisper: Now go to the light and let your life begin to unfold,
Angels have told.

Yevonne Tyus
*Mesa, AZ*

# Unrestrained Stupidity

Fellow Americans, please take heart.
Now is not the time to fall apart.
We've survived two great wars, the Great Depression,
and other periods of recession.

Don't look to others—we're all to blame.
The whole world bought into the game.
We bought, we sold—without a thought.
Now we must face what we have wrought.

No one group must bear the stain.
We all hopped on the gravy train.
It's cold comfort, we're not alone.
Millions stand to lose all they own.

With businesses closing one by one,
The fight for survival has only begun.
From CEO's to the littlest man,
We must each do what we can.

Perks and wages must be cut to the bone,
And some Union practices we dare not condone.
Cost must be effective in order to compete,
Or we may all end up on the street.

There is no magic potion to clean up this mess.
We must all work together and hope for the best.
"A penny saved is a penny earned,"
A wise old adage our parents learned.

Sharon H. Lund
*Ft. Pierce, FL*

## A Little Hug Is

A little hug is the affection of love
A little hug is like a hand in a glove
A little hug is the one that brings
A little hug is a new thing
Little hug, little hug
Little hug, little hug
A little hug is the thing in swing
A little hug is you create a ring
A little hug is the one we sing
A little hug is fit for a king
Little hug, little hug
Little hug, little hug
Little hug, little hug
Little hug, little hug
A little hug is the thing in swing
A little hug is you create a ring
A little hug is the funnest thing
A little hug is fit for a king
Little hug, little hug
Little hug, little hug
Little hug, little hug
Little hug, little hug

Anthony C. Romano
*Whiting, NJ*

# My Grandparents

God sent my grandparents to me, a gift from up above,
A true symbol of support and never-ending love.
I think about my grandparents nearly every day,
And I thank God for them every time I pray.

Nothing can compare to my grandparents' hugs.
Their arms are filled with warmth, encouragement, and love.
Years of wisdom and stories in their eyes,
I'm so thankful my grandparents are mine.

Now that I'm older and have known them longer,
We have a bond that is only getting stronger.
I recognize their importance and influence on me.
God's greatest gift has been my family.

At the end of the day, when I say my prayers at night,
I ask God to bless them and to hold them tight.
They are so special and mean very much to me.
They represent love and kindness and what we all are meant to be.

Amber Jarrett
*University Heights, OH*

# If I Could Fly

If I could fly up in the air,
do I dream or even dare?
Up above the trees so high,
I look down and see the sparrows
in the sky.
I see the grass so green below,
I hear my brother scream
away we go.
I spread my wings away I sail
In the distance I hear the town bell
I turn around
back home I go
Down, down, down
I sail so slow.
My mother says, lunch is ready for you.
Come in and be sure to wash up too.
My dream fades away, away they go.
Could I really fly?  No one knows.

Loise Everett
*Silver Creek, GA*

# Why Do I Feel this Way?

Why do I feel this way?
How can it be?
How can I tell him
About my other crush?
He knows I love him,
And he knows how much I care.
He needs to know the truth,
He needs to know who is involved.
I love you so much,
But there is another guy.
He took my heart,
But my heart is locked.
You have the key.
You've always had the key.
From the first day I saw you,
I knew it had to be.
I love you so much.
But you need to understand.
This other man
Has my heart.
Why can't you see?

Jessica R. Perry
*Chanute, KS*

# Not Good

Some people say that I am not good in anything I do,
And when I look back on everything sometimes I think it's true.
I'm not good in math.
I'm not good in speech.
I'm not good in foreign languages,
I have a C average in school at least.
I'm not good in writing.
I'm not good with words.
I'm not good in art,
And in dance I'm not good with salsa turns.
I'm not good in speed.
I'm not good with goodbyes.
I'm not good with death,
All I do is cry.
I'm not good in anything,
I'm not good I say,
But all of my friends are there to help me along the way.
So I may not be good at anything at all,
But all of you were there to catch me when I'd fall.

Angelina Zabala
*Buckeye, AZ*

Dreaming sometimes gives us the freedom to do the most amazing things. Each person has a passion or a desire that is indescribable to others but wonderful for that particular person. Hi, my name is Angelina Zabala and I am the author of "Dreaming of Freedom," my passion is to run. When I run it is a time when I don't have to worry about anything, when everything cycling in my head escapes me.

# Why Haven't I heard from You?

What did I do? Are you feeling blue? Did you meet someone new? Can
you give me a clue?

Strung out on dope? Unable to cope? Gave up all hope?
Visiting the pope?

Caught in a maze? Involved in a craze? Going through a phase?
Just in a daze?

Forgot my name? Found fortune and fame? Feeling some shame?
Merely playing a game?

Lacking motivation? Experiencing frustration? Discovered salvation?
Or unbridled procreation?

Hope you find this hilarious (even somewhat nefarious) with possibilities
endless and various, I'm left curious.

Carolyn Williams
*Woodbine, MD*

## Assisted Living Heebie-Jeebies

'Twas breezy and the slimy tomes
Did grind and frottage in my head
All flimsy were the bores in droves
And the home wrath outraged!
I do not wish to say a thing
'Cause it's so embarrassing
N'even for the big cha-ching
Do I want to say a thing
You, too, might get distraught
If foes were privy to your thought
However they do not distress
When taken for friendly witness
It comes in handy, not to frown
When something wrong is going down
Even if they're enemies
Their conscience guides them, anyways
It can make you really mean
If you get no ping in your peen
When I'm out of all recourse
I can be Chris Reeve's horse
To my detractors I say blast
I hope they're wiped clean as my ass
I really cover everything
I play piano and I sing
Lest you think I've gone and missed one
I'm not a kiss-ass, but a pissed one!

Robert Hyman
*N. Hollywood, CA*

## Back to Basics

Do you recall that God had a plan for humankind?
We were to procreate and also subdue the Earth
He gave us laws for our good that would bind
The whole world was filled with his joy and mirth

Then along came the enemy with his plan
He deceived the heart of this precious creature
Darkness and confusion settled over all the land
Man was left to choose his own teacher

God gave Man the strength to rise above it all
He gave us His attributes of faith, hope, and love
He promised to be there for us when we call
He said he would watch over us from above

Today our God is still awesome and living
Forget not our hearts are made for forgiving

Charlotte Vogel
*Warsaw, MO*

# Life

A star was sent for us to see
A man with God's knowledge
And the blessing we all need

As the world has dealt a bitter life to me
God awaits the better person inside of me He sees

I have wandered through this life of heartache with pain
Waiting God's word—with two remain
God's answers and patience for me
I hope for family faces and friends yet to see
For long ago, God's morals were to be erased
Now the so-called "professionals" have come to take their place

Our great nation has expanded and grown
However, this kind of greed just robs US ALL
History never learn, but Man has been told
That in God's hands the U.S. future He holds
Together we stand, but by greed we will fall

God has sent our answer
His Son for us all

Larry Craft
*Fairborn, OH*

## From My Window

I thought I saw a butterfly die today,
'Twas on the ground where I sprayed that it lay.
No longer would it flutter by;
I had not wanted it to die.
So out I went to pick it up,
But when I neared, it flew away,
'Twas then I said, "God bless the day."

Gladys P. Ziomek
*Tarpon Springs, FL*


## A Puppies Poem

I was in my front yard one day
When a small little dog strayed my way
He stood at my feet and looked up into my eyes
As if to say I am yours and you are mine
I reached down to pick him up
His fur is so soft and he was filled with so much love
I claimed him for my own
For I knew he hadn't a home
Oh all the fun times we had, so many of them
But now I am sad for God called him home
But yet I don't feel alone knowing that he is safe and free
Running through the tall green grass with all his friends
Knowing very well that someday we will all be together again

Renee Haupert
*Bremen, IN*

# Shelly and MeMe

"I'm pregnant" announced your mom,
I wanted to scream, but I stayed calm.
She was not married and very young,
"Help me" she said so I held my tongue.

God blessed us with a baby girl,
Welcome, little one, to the world,
As I looked into your sweet, little face,
All my fears and worries were erased.

A grandchild is the greatest gift
Of anything you could ever wish.
My life would never be the same,
Because MeMe is my new name.

How can I ever explain to you,
That all the things you say and do,
Make me so happy and give me such joy,
Just to sit and watch you play with a toy.

Shelly is a brown-eyed beauty,
Your dimples reveal such a cutie,
You amaze me because you are so smart,
I love you with all of my heart.

You are always in my thoughts,
I miss you when we're apart.
The bond we share will always be
Between Shelly and her MeMe.

Susan Schroader
*Louisville, KY*

## Summer

The warm dry air whisking away
My breath as dry as the air
The smell was like a summer flower
The trees as green as the grass
The sun shines on my face as I walk
The animals playing in the forest
The sun lowering down behind a hill
The sky as dark as a black hole
Now the air moist and fresh

Nikolos Buterakos
*Davison, MI*

## Gone

What I did I'll never know
What should have come will never show
You helped create a twin masterpiece
But shunned it after an eleven-year lease
The person I acknowledged as my hero
Soon became lower than a zero
The same person who filled me with so much anger
Became nothing more than a stranger
A single person in a pool of tears
A life destroyed in a matter of years
I listen to the sounds of a somber song
Seeing as though my life is gone

Trevahn Spearman
*Los Angeles, CA*

# A Silent Thought

In the absence of sound
A thought enters the core
Silence overwhelms
But the thought is so much more
Thinking and thinking
As the thought begins to fade
Trying to hold on as it slowly slips away
This thought must be important
But cannot be figured out
Still thinking and thinking
Frustration leads to a shout
As the thought has almost been cleared from the mind
A surge of energy makes it hard to hide
Continuing to think for the few moments left
It's all gone, nothing's left of the rest
The thought is gone
And is now filled with confusion
The thought is only an illusion
The silence fills one last time
Dissipates and leaves peace of mind

Stephanie Tarlton
*Rockford, IL*

## Marriage

This coveted day in one's life
Usually happens but once in their days
Uniting man and woman
To good fortune and luck in their ways
However, riding two on life's seat
A bump in the road may occur
But with God's blessing today
May their ride be secure

Vin Plagenza
*Enfield, CT*

## My Other Half

Life has been good
Life has been great
For I have found my perfect mate
Someone to share my life,
Someone to share the same path,
To share the same dreams, hopes
Together we will get by
Together we will grow old
Isn't life great
For I am not alone
I have my perfect mate

Ruth Goeden
*West Milwaukee, WI*

# The Veteran

He just came home
from war
in a miserable
mood
tired
depressed
by what he saw
men, women
and
children dying!
for what?
Why should his life
be distorted forever?
by constant memories of battles
popping up?
Day and night!
Why?

Anne Marfey
*Albany, NY*

# Woudda, Shoudda, Coudda

I woudda gladly married Warren,
But Mister Buffett never asked,
I woudda happily drunk with Dino,
But that wine remained uncasked.

I shoudda sung tunes with Frank,
Though my singing is not sweet,
Or I shoudda danced with Fred,
Though I have three left feet!

I coudda lived much differently
And enjoyed that richer style,
So I have hopes to reincarnate
And come back in a good while!

Marilyn A. Johnson
*Sebring, FL*

# The Written Word

Throughout my life
There has always been
The written words
Who were my friends.

They take me places
Where I want to be,
And show me things
I want to see.

Just like
A magic carpet ride
The book, a constant,
At my side.

To all those teachers
Of long ago,
I thank you for
The seeds of reading that you sowed.

The written word
How sweet you are,
The great escape
To all things far.

Leanora Salmon
*West Palm Beach, FL*

# Fire . . .

If I tore out my heart
      and handed it to you
Could you look inside and see
      the love it holds is true?
If I stood before you
      and wept a thousand tears
Or if I drove head first
      into all my fears!
If I stood before you and exposed my soul
or if I revealed to you that you make me whole
If I ripped open wide the flesh of my spine
could you tell that I am weak without you by my side?
If I stood before you and showed you my brain
would you still love me if I were insane?
If I were not uniquely me,
      by my side would you still be?

Katrina Hoskins
*Mineral Wells, TX*

# Woman's Reckoning "Tears"

By myself
All alone
Nobody else here at home
Not my sisters' pretty laughing faces
Not my precious children safely in their spaces
Just by myself
All alone
Not my husband to distract me
Nor my parents to detract me
Just by myself
All alone
All alone to accept the sadness
And let the tears flow
Just by myself
All alone
Finally free to let go

Kathleen Keegan
*Port St. Lucie, FL*

I'd been married for twenty-five years and went to therapy to see if I could save the marriage. I could not and this is how this poem came about.

# The Ballerina

Oh then dance the ballerina.
Dance with me!
So sweet as the honey
Made by the bees.

With a leap!
So high in the air,
You're so pretty,
We love all your flair.

Your pink posy pink tutus
Are from the fairies all around.
Your grace—like a swan's.
You dance to great sound.

Jill Astor
*Red Wing, MN*

## A Brush with Romance

Lost shadow in moon's silvery stream
We paint each a lover's dream
Each hath in mind this flame survives time
Our gladness be wild and troubles be few
Perennial as spring dew
Mist dances upon our lips
Our flesh doth thirst a tender kiss
Twilight sparks a passionate run
Two brushes become one
From a gentle touch new life begun
Escaping darkness into light
His sparkling eyes are blessed with sight
Small precious package sacred and new
Shall please Him as few do
We shall guide his way
Setting examples day by day
His future and spirit no one shall crush
A guarantee by his brush

Gary Maxwell
*Seattle, WA*

# Sweet Thoughts of You Grandmother

Sweet thoughts of you Grand Lady
touch my heart with tenderness
You've always been my anchor
kept my life from sailing amiss

You taught me with your wisdom
your hands guiding all the way
Through time of stormy weather
your love shone as bright sunrays

My one true inspiration
for learning right from wrong
To you I looked, Grandmother
for the strength to carry on

And always when my sadness
became more than I could bear
there was you to bring me comfort
with your love you'd dry my tears

You're a very special part of me
in you I found such a pleasure
I cherish the lifetime of memories
each thought of you a treasure

Judith A. Letizio
*Wooster, OH*

## Jack Frost

Jack Frost took his paintbrush
As he sailed across the sky,
So every morning when the sun comes up
His artwork greets the eye.

There're reds and golds and yellows,
All of a breathtaking view,
But no matter how hard he tries,
He can never make the leaves turn blue.

So when you're in bed sleeping,
And outside everything seems faint,
Just remembering at midnight,
Jack Frost begins to paint.

Carl Jessee
*Pennington Gap, VA*

## Birthday Blues

I'm feeling awfully bad today, you see, it's my birthday and I'm 83!
I've lived too long, my song is sung, I climbed the ladder rung by rung.
I tasted life, some good, some bad and hard times,
it seemed I always had.
But wonderful days I've also seen, sometimes so real, sometimes just a
dream.
When life's pathway got too hard to walk, I learned one thing is cheap,
And that is talk.
I talked to the stars, sisters and brothers—my talks proved love for each
other.
Still sad, I look up and see clouds drifting by, then see the stars bright in
the sky. I really began to wonder, why?
Then I look at my son, honest and shy but so strong—
I see my daughter now, so brave and sweet.
Suddenly my heart eases—I see everything I've done is not all wrong.
Do I wish these years when I've grown so old,
Had given more, such as silver and gold?
No, as I look deep within my soul, I know I've really reached my goal.
Had I not lived to this ripe old age, look at all I would have missed . . .
I would never have known the sweetness of grandkids, even great-
grandbabies, never would have felt their precious hug or kiss—
Yes, life sure can get us down, but now, since I've really thought it
through,
83 is really kind of great—I feel pretty good. So I will treat myself
To a cup of coffee and have a birthday doughnut, too!

Juanita Seeley
*Clarinda, IA*

I have worked in nursing nearly all of my working years. I have two wonderful children—a son and a daughter—six grandchildren and four precious great-grandchildren. I have two wonderful sisters and one brother—many nieces and nephews—relatives and friends. I am now eighty-three years old. I was born in Clarinda, Iowa in the ghetto area called Guntown. How wonderful we never get too old to learn. I have learned the answer to most of our heartaches and problems. The answer is love!

# Touching

If my heart could sing
And could be free
If my soul reached out
From melancholy

If my eyes took on
What I could see
If my spirit
Would let me be

Then opened wide
My spirit soar
Big and deep
Would be the door.

Joette Montgomery
*Chandler, AZ*

## Our Cold Land

The white flakes upon the land,
The dark clouds drift across the sky.
The birds are finding food for the winter
While the snow is drifting on by.
I see a little animal going underground
With their feet tapping on the ground.
And when the snow begins to melt and the rivers are rising high,
I see people coming back out and reaching for the sky.

Kristin
*Hibbing, MN*

I am single and I have no children. I enjoy writing poetry and have been writing for thirteen years. I live in Northeastern Minnesota.

# Burlesque

To see her dancing on the stage
The curtain draws, and she appears
Draped in feathers, wearing lace

Her heels, her strut, rogue on her face
The way she teases makes me stare
To see her dancing on the stage

She moves with such a flowing grace
Her wardrobe planned with greatest care
Draped in feathers, wearing lace

The corset loosened from her waist
Amidst the whistling and the cheers
To see her dancing on the stage

The cheers grow louder in this place
Her breasts emerge from her brassiere
Draped in feathers, wearing lace

The show goes on, it's getting late
Time well spent to watch her here
To see her dancing on the stage
Draped in feathers, wearing lace

Emiliano Lebron
*Ashtabula, OH*

# What Is Love

Oh mother, how I love that man
He is so sweet, so tender
He brings out the woman in me

That car is beautiful
The color, the style, that new car smell
Oh, how I love everything about it

It's so roomy, rooms are beautiful
The spot, the neighborhood, schools, church so near
I really love that house

Eyes blue, hair blonde, skin so soft, angelic face
He looks like his father, as sweet as me
My first born, oh how I love him

The man, the car, the house, the baby
All are expressions of love

So what is love?

Is it a state of mind that is never understood?

Chris White
*Callao, VA*

# Toes on the Edge

She stands on the edge of the cliff overlooking the great ocean, her toes touch the edge. She was stripped of everything in her life. She only has her heart and soul and the emptiness that fills her. Heart and soul fight the emptiness. She calls upon her angels to save her but she hears no answer. Toes on the edge, she awaits the answers as the tears fall down her face. She cries out, if my toes leave the edge will you lift me or if my toes leave the edge will you let me fall? The angel speaks. You must know who you are. You did not fight your whole life to just fall. Your toes do not have to leave the edge to fly, you are not empty because you have your heart and soul. When you look to the stars or the morning sky, a bird or another person's smile, this will find you. We all feel broken at times. We must remember we are all surrounded by angels. We only have to reach out. They are listening and give the answers we so desperately need. She looks for a miracle to save her. The true miracle is life, the answers are all around you. The secret that nature brings is a rebirth every day, she wants to smile a real smile through the pain, she stays positive and optimistic. There is real happiness. She is waiting and searching. Her journey has been very sad, but she will smile and will find herself. Answers within herself and with the guide of her angels she will fly again and will be broken no more.

Carol A. Leveski
*Almont, MI*

# In Memoriam to Lexia

A precious little bundle came down from up above,
Delivered by the angels, to you, from God with love.
And fastened to the blanket by a slender silken thread
Gently tucked within the folds, was a golden card which read,

"Please care for her and love her and treasure every smile,
For I'll be back to claim her in just a little while.
Enjoy each fleeting moment and every passing hour,
For soon this tender bud will be a full-blown flower."

"In our heavenly garden there's not one bloom to spare
Every single blossom receives such loving care.
Tended by the angels, adored by those below
This special heavenly garden sets Earth's black night aglow.

So raise your eyes toward Heaven and view that land afar,
And may your heart find comfort as you behold the brightest star."

Donna J. Goss-Deck
*Pleasant Gap, PA*

# My Dad and I

Dad was in the Naval Reserve when I was born.
So I saw his uniform weekly worn.
It looked so sharp and he stood so tall,
Being proud of what he learned and all.
When Dad made Chief it was no wonder
He attended meetings faithfully without a blunder.
His Chief's uniform had a different look,
Suit, hat, collar devices, like in a book.
So at fourteen, I knew what I had to do!
See the world and save my country too.
I wanted to look just like that,
So I hurried up the ladder like a Navy brat,
took every Navy course that I could find,
Making Chief being first on my mind.
So here I am, today's my day,
Another Chief has made their way.
I'm happy as can be, hoping Dad is proud of me.
He's the best Chief the Navy ever did see.
Now they've pinned the second best—me!
Today we can look at each other and say,
God bless the Navy and the USA.

Sheila Miller
*Van Dyne, WI*

I wrote this poem when my daughter, Sue made Chief Petty Officer in the U.S. Navy.

# My Hero

You were the one that brought me
out of the dark abyss.
You were the one who taught me
to love.
You were the one I looked to
for support.
You were the one that helped me
get through so much.
Thanks for being there
My hero
My love
My best friend
My everything.
You were the one that
put the pieces of my heart back together.
You were the only one that
could see into my soul.
You were the one that I wanted forever.
Thanks for being there
My hero
My love
My soul mate
My everything.
Please don't leave me now that I need you.
I do need you.
I love you.

Kayla Stoutenborough
*Washington, IL*

# We Need a Change

We need a change
in this life.
This is the time
the world needs
to get better.
We need a change,
crime at a young age.
Death happening every day.
What are we to do?
What are we to say?
We need a change.
Too many people on the street.
We need to start to think.
We can help if we try.
This way no child
will need to cry
that they lost their folks
or they live on the street
with no food, no shoes on their feet.
We need to change,
maybe it will start with this
simple poem and rhyme.
We know we can do this!
Someday, maybe,
it will start right now today.

Jason Knutson
*Bemidji, MN*

# Trust

They say they trust you
But they really don't
They say they'll hold you
But you know they won't

They say they'll listen
But they don't care
I know you trust them
But you don't get your fair share

They say they'll help you
But they never do
Trust is a choice for everyone
And it's up to you too

They say they'll cry with you
But their eyes are really dry
They say they're gonna leave you
And right there, you want to die

Jesenia Molina
*Camden, NJ*

# In the Garden

When winter is over and spring is here,
I head to the garden—a place so dear.
I start the tiller and plow the soil;
It's a lot of work—but enjoyable toil.
To plant the seeds and watch them grow,
It's a magical thing, everyone should know.
Plowing and planting is merely a start;
You'll do much more if you're really smart.
Use fertilizer and a good sharp hoe—
Get to the task when grass and weeds grow.
As summer comes and it gets hotter,
If rain is scarce—you may need to water.
You'll get onions, tomatoes and corn;
There's something to pick almost every morn.
Beans, peas, and squash come on the vine;
The eating they provide is very fine.
Cucumbers, melons, and okra will appear;
If you can't eat it all . . . well, never fear.
Can some, freeze some, or give it away;
You might even find someone willing to pay.
A garden gives exercise and good eating;
Better start early—the season is fleeting.
It's a pleasure working the ground;
A better pastime I've never found.

Bill E. Ramsey
*Covington, TX*

# Bridges

Something in us loves to build a bridge,
To send out filaments of steel or stone
Or structured sound to span the emptiness
Between two worlds that could or should be one.

The bridge across a river or a sea
Is easiest to build, for banks will bear
The weight of steely beams and cables—all
That's needed to complete a thoroughfare.

But those frail bridges spun of sound like
"This I need" or "That I know" or "You I love"
Are miracles of engineering skill.
They join, with only vowels and consonants,
The shifting shores of separate minds and hearts.

Such builders weave of words a cable strong
Enough to shuttle weightiest thoughts across
Vast gulfs of darkness—racing back and forth
Like lighted trains at night on tracks of sound.

William J. Dusel
*Los Gatos, CA*

# Reach Out

I feel so very blessed today.
I know it's from all the prayers I say.
Our sweet Lord is always there
To give us hope and strength to share.
Helping one another in that special way
Can get us through a trying day.
I feel that I should give what I can
And be there for my fellow man.
If someone is hungry, I really feel
They should be given a friendly meal.
Sometimes people aren't there enough.
Usually when times get rough.
Giving should just come without a thought.
That's not something we should have to be taught.
Sometimes kind words or a caring smile
Is all someone needs to feel worthwhile.

Jennifer VanHarlingen
*Cocoa, FL*

## You at End of Light

I've been crying as seasons pass
Time stands still, I've lost my past
Will you be there standing with open arms
Or let me slip away as the years travel on?
Hiding my secrets looking for a way
To break my chains walking in circles
Just letting me slip away
I keep believing in you and what will be
Hoping things get better as life blows through the trees
It feels like I'm cut to pieces left in silence
Praying you never feel the pain I have suffered
Into nowhere pushing forward
Wondering what I'll discover
Please let me find you at the end of the light

Nikkie Boling
*Nitro, WV*

# The Angel in You

Everyone's special
In their different ways,
Do not waste them
And you'll find the angel in you.

Keep your head up
And remember to stay strong,
Do not think the worst
And you'll find the angel in you.

Whenever you feel
The darkness inside.
Remove it all
To find the angel in you.

Guilt is a boulder
It can weigh you down.
Don't let it take over
So you'll find the angel in you.

To know the right path
Think of the possibilities,
Listen to your heart
And find the angel in you.

The angel in you
Is a special feeling
That lives in your soul
And lifts you from the ground.

Benjamin L. Strickland
*Stedman, NC*

I was born on June 12, 1992, and raised with my family in a small town called Stedman, North Carolina. When I was in the eighth grade I learned about poetry. One Valentine's Day, in my drama class, my teacher talked about similes and metaphors. A year later, just weeks before Christmas, I decided to write a Christmas poem. I though it was a good experience. I read it to one of my friends and she encouraged me to write more. At that time I started writing more poetry and even wrote an entire book of poetry based on experiences I had in high school. This poem discusses feelings you shouldn't have.

# Rose

Rose is a many splendid thing
It's a name that's like no other
It's a beautiful fragrant flower
It's a tender loving mother.

Rose is as soft as velvet
When it sparkles with the dew
It reminds me so much Mother
Just how much I love you.

Rose embraces the sunlight
Its petals open wide.
Gathering in all the warmth
The sunlight can provide.
Your arms are like that, Mother
When you hold me close inside.
Giving my heart a refuge,
A safe warm place to hide.

Paulette Robinson
*Leicester, NC*

# The Engagement

His voice sounded so excited,
What he had to say couldn't possibly wait
He knew how he felt about her
It was love, from their very first date

He called and wanted our "blessing"
Before he asked our daughter to be his wife
He said that he loved her more than anything
And wanted to be with her the rest of his life

Our main concern is our daughter's happiness
Were the words that her daddy shared
Then he told of his love for our daughter
You could just tell how much he cared

We were so proud of his manners
It showed he was a respectful man
We each gave him our blessing
For the young man to take our daughter's hand

We could have searched the whole world over
To find our daughter's true love
But here he is right before us
The man she has always dreamed of

Brenda J. Hill
*Piedmont, MO*

My husband Tom and I have one beautiful daughter. Her name is Sarah Beth. Sarah became engaged on Valentine's Day 2007. With her wedding engagement I wanted to give her something special. I wanted her to always have the words from my heart. Our daughter is truly a blessing to us from God. With love always, Momma.

# Untitled

I mined a mine,
It seemed to seem
To find some ore,
Or what it means
I mined this vein in vain 'tis true.
The lode I load was you, not ewe.

The lamb who took it on the lam,
Did not cotton to be a spam.
But for the dough the frisky doe
Took on a deer whose price was dear.

Not so the steer who waxed austere,
And was not cowed by cows it's clear,
Because there was no udder way
To utter oaths for oats or hay.

Now if these odes give off an odor
Distinct that permeates the air.
Consider the poet and bestow it,
Give credit to their rightful heir.
Call me Shakespeare if you will,
For Will it is that fills the bill.

Take not from me my memories dear,
For they are treasured souvenirs.
We call back fondly times of yore,
Because those times come back no more,
Except we keep them live you see,
In cobwebbed diary . . . memories.

Frank M. Carafano
*Handen, CT*

# Untitled

Na Ni and Tha Thi were one of a kind,
all that they did was for their children in mind.
Ten did they raise, seven girls, and three boys.
Through all those hard depression days,
We all grew up and had children of our own.
To the delight of Na Ni and Tha Thi to see
what they had sown.
Their eyes and their smile lit up when we visited,
Then sadness came over them when we exited.
The meals that they made were the best ever had.
While we were there everyone was glad.
We all have to go to the place of our rest.
All was sad still—Na Ni and Tha Thi were the best.

Michael A. Longo, Sr.
*Hazelton, PA*

What inspired me the most when I wrote this poem was the great amount of love and
sacrifice my parents made. They raised a large family during the depression years of the
1930s. My father was unemployed and did odd jobs he could find until he went to work
with the N.P.A. that President Roosevelt started. My mother worked in a dress factory
for ten cents an hour, yet we never went to bed hungry. There were many other wants
that were never gotten but we lived through it all with love and support from our parents
first and then from all of my siblings. I've since lost my parents and four sisters and I
dedicate this poem to them.

# Index of Poets

Pulley, Nancy 126

# R

Rae, Robin 147
Rae, Susanna-Judith 292
Ragsdell, Betty 339
Ramsey, Bill E. 376
Ramsey, Zach 124
Reagan, Ryan J. 237
Reckelhoff, Brett 274
Redman, Ferol 175
Reese, Alice A. 188
Reilly, Madge 151
Renna, Audrey A. 176
Reyes, Larry M. 100
Reynoso, Bryan 131
Rice, Susan 118
Richardson, Diana 76
Ridge, Janice 168
Riggins, Dorothy 66
Rinaldi, Stephanie 175
Rios, Edwin 207
Rivera, Clarissa 53
Rizzotto, Rosemary 307
Robinson, Paulette 381
Rodgers, Venora 136
Rodriguez, Maria 314
Romano, Anthony C. 342
Rosa, Felipe 308
Rushing, Willie E. 90

# S

Saberin, Paul 214
Salmon, Leanora 358
Sarracino, Justin 305
Sauers, James 69
Schlauraff, Kristie A. 226
Schroader, Susan 352
Schuetz, Gary A. 262
Schwedler, Susan E. 9
Scott, Micahh 75
Scrantz, Alissa 231
Sedeno, Michelle L. 333
Seeley, Juanita 365

Seely, Faith 181
Seifert, Amanda 42
Shepherd, Debbie D. 146
Shifflett, Kasey G. 4
Shirley, Lesley S. 127
Shyne, Michelle E. 303
Sickler, Marie 324
Silver, Lauren 203
Sisk, Ricky L. 328
Skatula, Debbie 228
Slavich, Caitlyn 135
Smart, Dominique 180
Smirnes, Shari A. 283
Smith, Kalonie 22
Smith, Lois A. 133
Smith, Mary L. 68
Smith, Renee 92
Smith, Shawnice 286
Sparks, Michael D. 24
Spearman, Trevahn 353
Specht, Abby 171
Spencer, Suzanne 170
Stadalis, Jeffery C. 248
Stalvey, Allyson B. 148
Stammer, Ross G. 13
Staton, Chandra 149
Steagall, Tabbitha K. 283
Stein, Arthur 306
Steinhaus, Tab F. 178
Stephens, Kenneth 280
Stopa, Franciszka 188
Stoutenborough, Kayla 373
Strickland, Benjamin L. 380
Studnicky, Julie 48
Suckow, Laura 98
Swick, Lee Ann 235

# T

Tam, Sau K. 93
Tamayo, Stephanie 270
Tarlton, Stephanie 354
Taylor, Danielle 218
Thielman, Morgan 197
Thomas, Jincy 197

Breinigsville, PA USA
29 August 2009
223119BV00003B/2/P